The Calling *of a* Part-Time *Pastor*

A
Guidebook
For Small
Church
Leaders

WARREN SEIBERT

WESTBOW
PRESS®
A DIVISION OF THOMAS NELSON
& ZONDERVAN

WestBow Press books may be ordered through booksellers or by contacting:

WestBow Press
A Division of Thomas Nelson & Zondervan
1663 Liberty Drive
Bloomington, IN 47403
www.westbowpress.com
1 (866) 928-1240

ISBN: 978-1-5127-4838-3 (sc)
ISBN: 978-1-5127-4839-0 (e)

Print information available on the last page.

WestBow Press rev. date: 7/26/2016

Dedicated to

my wife Ruth,
and the members of the
West Copake Reformed Church,

for your partnership in the gospel.

Forward

We are so easily seduced by the standards of the world. The world judges success in a material way. How much money do you make? How big is the corporation? How many square feet is your home? How many people serve under you?

In the church, we can easily succumb to that idolatry. How big is your church? How many parking spaces? How many people at worship Sunday mornings? What is your budget?

Those are human standards, not divine. The Word of God corrects this mistake in Deuteronomy, chapter 7. There we read, "For you are a people holy to the LORD your God. The LORD your God has chosen you to be people for his treasured possession, out of all the peoples who are on the face of the earth. It was not because you were more in number than any other people that the LORD set his love on you and chose you, for you were the fewest of all peoples, but it is because the LORD loves you and is keeping the oath that he swore to your fathers..." God chooses whom He chooses, based not on human standards, but on His own.

Pastor Warren has a heart for ministry in small churches. *The Calling of a Part-Time Pastor* is written for all leaders of small churches. This guidebook is a gateway into fully understanding the trials and joys of working together to lead your small church to fulfill your calling in Jesus Christ. The insights you will discover on these pages will help you to make the best, most bilblical decisions as you seek to call a part-time pastor to your church. So valuable is the guidance you will receive in this book that I urge your leaders to read it before looking for a minister, while the search is being conducted, and once again when the task is complete. If you use this book as a guide, you will find help in making the future ministry of your church the very best it can be.

This book is also for ministers considering a call to a small church. Here you will be reminded of what you already know—that your ministry matters!—and that small churches matter in the kingdom of God. This book will resonate with what is in your heart and mind about Jesus Christ. *The Calling of a Part-Time Pastor* will elevate you in your calling, reminding you that your service and your church is holy and indispensable, and will serve as a valuable guide to effective and faithful part-time or bivo-cational ministry.

Its author is a man who has revitalized every church he has served. Warren is an extraordinary pastor. What is it about him that has led his churches all to grow under his leadership? You will find that out for yourself as you read: The secret to Warren's pastoral leadership is it's rootedness in the gospel. He knows whom he serves and why he serves.

In a time when the church is casting about hoping for revival, Pastor Warren is convinced that it is to be found in ministers and lay leaders who know whom they serve and why they serve. Those pastors and leaders must have a vital relationship with our Risen, living Lord. That is the key to a living, thriving church.

Worthy is the lamb! This must be proclaimed in a church regardless of size. Pastor Warren shows us how this can be. In these pages we learn that small churches matter. Faithfulness in ministry and witness is not about size, it is about the center. Is your church built on the rock? (Matt 7:24)

Rev. Dr. Fred Mueller
Millstone, New Jersey
Easter 2016

CONTENTS

INTRODUCTION

Leading a small church is no small task. This is as true for the elders and the deacons of a small church as it is for any pastor. There is work to be done, important work for God, but there is usually a limited supply of people and resources available to accomplish our mission. Almost everything—from volunteers to staff a Sunday School to paper towels for the kitchen—seems to be in short supply.

However true this is, in many small churches today, Jesus is glorified. Lives are being changed. People are being cared for. Spiritual growth is taking place. Even the bills are getting paid. Faith, hope, and love are present in abundance. God is magnificently at work in our midst.

Yes, even in small churches. In fact, the majority of Protestant churches in North America today—nearly 2/3 of them—are what we would describe as small churches, with less than 100 in average attendance at worship.[1] There are more than 100,000 churches in the United States with

---

[1] David R. Ray, *The Indispensable Guide for Smaller Churches* (Cleveland, OH: Pilgrim Press, 2003), xi.

less than 50 people in their Sunday morning service.[2] It is believed that more people today make the small church their spiritual home than any other size church in this country, making it the "dominant institutional expression of Protestant Christianity in America."[3]

This means, of course, that small churches are not unusual. And they are certainly not a mistake. They are established by God, sustained by God, and dearly loved by God. As the saying goes, "God must love small churches— since we have so many of them!"

Here is the bottom line: Small churches are churches too! If we are faithful to the mission that God has given us then we are a church. Period. The size of the congregation doesn't determine the health of the church. Neither does the height of the steeple, the amount of spaces in the parking lot, or the number of children in the Sunday school. Really. Even having no Sunday school does not determine the health of a church. How can I say that? Simply because having a Sunday School in the church was not a common feature of any congregation until well into the 19th century. They are actually a new thing—like organ music and hymnals—just not as new as guitars, drums, and projectors. The only thing that really matters in determining whether a church is healthy or not is our

[2] Dennis Bickers, The Healthy Small Church (Kansas City, MO: Beacon Hill, 2005), 13.

[3] Lyle Schaller, The Small Membership Church: Scenarios for Tomorrow (Nashville, TN: Abington, 1994), 12.

love of the Lord and fulfilling our calling to be the kind of church that Jesus desires us to be. Not even having a "full-time" pastor is a requirement for church health, as we will soon see.

Every local church, no matter what size it may be, has been called by God to the same essential ministries—such as worship, fellowship, discipleship, and evangelism. The words we use to describe this mission aren't really as important as the commitment we have to glorifying God, to caring for those in need, to loving one another in the church, to growing together in faith, and to sharing the gospel in our community. These are what a healthy church does—whether we have paid staff, established committees, or lines in our budgets for these ministries or not.

Yet, it is essential to point out, although this is what all healthy churches do, the way in which we "do church" is unique for each congregation. Not only is the faith and life of a local church shaped by the heritage, traditions and particular experiences of that congregation, but each church has specific challenges to overcome depending upon the size of their membership. In other words, small churches are not "little" big churches. "They are different orders of God's creation," as someone once said.[4] They can't be governed, grown or lead in the same way as a larger church; not only will the leaders of the church become frustrated, discouraged, and perhaps burned-out if we try to, but the mission

---

[4] Schaller, 135.

of the church will suffer, eventually becoming inefficient or ineffective in our calling as a church.

This is why the calling of a pastor for a small church is no small task either. It is a unique calling for a pastor. This is especially the case when the situation of the church requires them to call a "part-time" pastor. To be honest, many churches do not know what are the special challenges, demands, stresses, and rewards that a "part-time" pastor must face. And quite frankly, even the pastors often have no idea what leading a small church is like before they accept the call—and often for a long time after that. This was certainly true in my case. Unfortunately, many "part-time" pastors don't seem to stick around long enough to ever find out; if they did, I am certain that a great many of them would grow to appreciate and enjoy their calling.

This is why this guide has been prepared. It is offered to church leaders who are in the process of calling a "part-time" pastor for their church. I also have in mind pastors who are considering a call to a small church in a less than "full-time" capacity. I believe they can also gain a much needed perspective from the discussion to follow, one that will both enhance their pastorate and enable them to feel fulfilled as ministers in this unique and often misunderstood role.

At present, 30% of all Protestant churches are served by "part-time" pastors.[5] This number is expected to grow

---

[5] Hartford Seminary, "2010 Faith Communities Today Survey" as reported by Jeffrey MacDonald, "Churches Turn to Part-Time Clergy" in *Christian Century* (September 18, 2013), 16-17.

considerably in the coming years.[6] Even many churches with around 100 people in average worship attendance will move toward calling a "part-time" pastor due to the ever-increasing financial challenges of meeting the salary, housing, pension, and health insurance costs involved in supporting a "full-time" minister.[7]

I write to you as a "part-time" pastor in a small church. I also write to you as someone who loves small churches. I was raised in a small church, joined a small church as an adult, was ordained in a small church, and began my life as an ordained minister in a small church. And when I say small, I mean that every one of these churches had an average worship attendance of less than 100 people when I started, often much less. But every one of these churches was strong in faith, hope, and love. I thank the Lord for all of them.

I have also been blessed with the opportunity to be a pastor in a "middle" size church and to serve in a contract status with a "large" church as a pastoral counselor. I appreciate these ministries as well and sincerely believe that God is in the midst of all faithful churches whatever their size or shape may be. But I also say, without apology, that the small church has always been my spiritual family and will likely always have my heart.

As I said, I am a "part-time" pastor in a small church.

---

[6] Schaller, 12-13.

[7] Dennis Bickers, *The Work of the Bivocational Minister* (Valley Forge, PA: Judson Press, 2007), 18-19.

You may have noticed that I have been writing "part-time" with quotation marks. I will stop doing this soon. The reason I have been putting "part-time" in quotes is because we often call this position "part-time" when, in fact, I don't believe there is such a creature as a "part-time" pastor. I am not ¾ of a pastor, or ½ of a pastor, or ¼ of a pastor. The truth is, there is not a moment of my life when I do not think of myself as *the* pastor of the church I serve. When I am in the church building leading worship, I am the pastor of the church. When I am having supper with my family, I am still the pastor of the church. Even when I am working at my other vocation, I am still the pastor of the church. And I am glad my church thinks this way too. I am with them week by week, in word and sacrament, as their pastor. I am on-call for them as their pastor 24/7—like any other pastor. The only thing that is really "part-time" or *partial* about my ministry position is the amount of financial compensation that my church is able to provide at this time.

This is why I prefer the term "bivocational" to describe my life and service to our Lord and his churches, and why you will see me use this term interchangeably with part-time pastor in what follows. Simply defined, *a bivocational pastor is someone serving in a ministry setting who must rely upon an additional source of income outside that ministry in order to support themselves or their family.* This would include a pastor who must rely upon the health benefits supplied by a spouse's employer since, without this assistance, the pastor could not serve that church with the salary that church alone provides.

Of course, this is not the only kind of part-time pastor we will find serving in small churches. We also see pastors who have retired from full-time—or fully compensated—ministries who still feel the call of God to serve in a local church. We also know that there are pastors who serve in more than one local church, sharing their gifts and time between two or more churches. Although I will briefly touch on these possible candidates for small churches seeking to call a part-time pastor, I will mostly spend our time together considering the typical challenges to overcome and the true pitfalls to avoid as you consider calling a bivocational pastor for your church.

To this end, I share with you my own experience as a person who grew up and came of age in small churches and who is now serving as a bivocational pastor. I have also drawn from conversations with small churches leaders I have had throughout the years, with part-time pastors I have interviewed, from discussions with denominational representatives, and from a host of written resources I have consulted and sometimes argued with over the course of my ministry. All have contributed to what I share with you now.

This guidebook is divided in three parts. In the first part, "The World of *Part-Time* Ministry," chapter 1 explores the biblical and historical context of this form of ministry and places your local church right in the mix of the great things the Lord has been accomplishing through small churches from the beginning of the church to our present day. In chapter 2, the calling of all Christians to ministry in the church, pastors and church members alike, is presented. Please don't skip over this section—it sets the foundation for everything that follows. I have found this material not only revealing, but exciting and spiritually encouraging. Even more, I believe what is most essential for many small church leaders today is a new perspective, a new way of seeing small churches in light of our significant and historical role in the kingdom of God.

In part two, "The World of the *Part-Time* Church," we take a close look at the mission of the church and the role of every believer within the church, including the pastor. Chapter 3 presents what the Word of God says a "church" is meant to be and do, and significantly, what a "part-time church" really is. (Notice the quotes!) Chapter 4 then presents what the Bible reveals about the person and work of the pastor, paying particular attention to what this looks like for a part-time pastor.

The third part, "A Partnership in *Full-Time* Ministry," is meant to get us really rolling up our sleeves and doing the work of improving the process of calling a part-time pastor to a church, so a healthy and fruitful ministry will result. In chapter 5, several expectations for the pastor and the church—realistic or otherwise—are discussed, including my suggestions for developing mutual expectations that will define and enhance the ministry of every church with a bivocational pastor. Then, chapter 6 outlines the essential areas that must be addressed by all church leaders—pastors, search committees, consistories, supervisors—in order to better serve part-time pastors and their churches.

Each part ends with a section that provides questions for reflection or discussion with a group. What I have in mind is a group of leaders in a church or members of a pastoral search committee getting together to reflect, discuss, and pray through these sections over several weeks *before* even a single candidate is interviewed. This is just a suggestion, of course, but I believe you will find this process fruitful.

Throughout this work, we will speak openly about some of the difficulties many small churches have in adjusting to having a bivocational pastor as well as several traits that make leading a small church much different than other churches. The presence of a bivocational pastor in your church does mean that changes must take place in the life and work of the congregation for you to be a healthy church and for you to continue to fulfill your God-given mission just like you desire. I promise you this: These changes are not catastrophic changes, they are not disruptive changes, and they have the potential of making your church even more healthy, fulfilling, and enjoyable than it is right now.

What you will not find in these pages is a procedure manual for pastoral search committees describing the various steps to take to successfully call a pastor—from doing a church study and writing a church profile to interviewing candidates and issuing a call. These types of manuals already exist and are readily available from many denominations and in many Christian book stores. But what they all seem to lack, to one degree or another, is an awareness of the specific needs of a small church seeking to call a part-time pastor. To be fair, they weren't written to address these issues. So what follows is meant to supplement or add to the valuable guidance these manuals do provide.

It is my ardent prayer and urgent hope that God may be glorified and that your church may be blessed by this offering.

QUESTIONS FOR REFLECTION

1. *What does it mean to you that more people call a small church their spiritual home than any other size church in this country?*

2. *Does the size of a congregation determine the health of a church? If not, what does?*

3. *Can a church be healthy and growing with a "part-time" pastor? Why or why not?*

Part One:
THE WORLD OF PART-TIME MINISTRY

Chapter 1
A Firm Foundation

My church believes they have been around for nearly 2000 years. They believe it because this is precisely what I keep telling them. Although our church began to worship together over 250 years ago on the spot of ground where our building stands today, that wasn't the actual origin of our church's life. Not even close.

If we go back just a few years before that, another church in our area felt the leading of the Holy Spirit to plant our church several miles down the road from where they were gathering in worship so that the settlers who were beginning to occupy our section of the region didn't have to travel so far on foot or by buggy-ride to attend public worship. As it happens, that church was founded by a group of previous settlers a generation before, many of whom were new to our country, building their church even as they were building their own homes and farms in the community. And why did they want to build their church? Because people in their homeland once built a community of faith back there, shared with them the

1

gospel of Jesus Christ, and they believed they were called by God to do the same where they were living and working now.

Yet, even before that, believers shared their faith in the Lord with the people of their homeland. They heard it from others, many years before that. One generation, one group of people, witnessing to their faith and handing down the gospel throughout the years, even as they had received eternal life. If we keep tracing this stream of faith back through the years, we will discover that it all flows from the testimony of those who first walked with our Lord Jesus, who is himself the true Source of our faith and life as a church today.

HISTORICAL ROOTS

The same is true for your congregation. The Source of your church can be traced all the way back to Jesus, the "living water," who gave your church life and purpose. (John 4:7-15; 7:37-39). Furthermore, the mission of all our churches remains the same now as it was in the beginning. Hear the words of our Lord Jesus in the Great Commandment and the Great Commission:

> *You shall love the Lord your God with all your heart and with all your soul and with all your mind. This is the great and first commandment. And the second is like it: You shall love your*

neighbor as yourself. On these two command-ments depend all the Law and the Prophets.

-Matthew 22:37-40

Go therefore and make disciples among the na-tions, baptizing them in the name of the Father and of the Son and of the Holy Spirit, teaching them to observe all I have commanded you. And behold, I am with you always, to the end of the age.

-Matthew 28:19-20

What is remarkable to me is how the church was able to carry out this purpose without all the modern ameni-ties, equipment, techniques, and facilities that we often think are essential to having a strong and healthy church. Compared to us, they had very little. A small group of people, stepping out in faith to follow in the way of Jesus, were used by our Lord to proclaim the gospel of salvation, to plant and build churches, to grow communities of be-lievers that would eventually lead to the establishing of your church and my church for today.

Few of these churches had a full-time pastor. When we look back to the churches in the New Testament, there is no evidence of any pastor being what we would call "full-time" or "fully compensated" by a church for their labors.[8] Nor were there any large congregations. Sometimes, when we read the book of Acts, we can get the impression that on the day of Pentecost a church of 3000 people came into existence by the Holy Spirit through the preaching of Peter. True, that did happen (Acts 2:41). But these new believers didn't remain in Jerusalem to form the first "mega-church" in history. After the festival of Pentecost was over, many of them returned to their homelands, bringing the gospel with them. These early Christians then established small churches in their region, often meeting together in homes for worship, fellowship, and prayer. Some of those who did remain in Jerusalem didn't linger there for long; persecutions sent them out throughout the Middle East and Europe as witnesses to Jesus Christ where other small churches were formed. The book of Acts records this story. It is our story.

The apostle Paul worked as a tentmaker while planting and leading some of these churches (Acts 13:3, 2 Thes 3:7-8). For this reason, the apostle Paul is often called the "Father of Bivocational Pastors."[9] Even so, the apostle Paul was not the first or the last bivocational pastor in the church. In fact—please hear this—it was the dominant form of ministry in the early church and remained the "norm" for pastoral ministry all throughout church his-

---

[8] Os Guiness, *The Call: Finding and Fulfilling the Central Purpose of Your Life* (Nashville, TN: Thomas Nelson, 2003), 49.

[9] Luther Dorr, *The Bivocational Pastor* (Nashville, TN: Broadman, 1988), 7.

tory up to the 20ᵗʰ century.[10] Even though many in our contemporary church perceive bivocational ministry as a new trend—or a new problem!—that the church has to acknowledge, study, and overcome today, the truth is that part-time pastors are not a new phenomenon at all, but have always existed and have always provided a vital and fruitful ministry in the name of Jesus Christ. In fact, a careful study of church history demonstrates that what is actually "new" in the church is full-time clergy. Even today, the majority of pastors serving the churches throughout the world are part-time pastors.[11]

A careful review of the history of my own denomination, the Reformed Church in America, reveals many important, but long overlooked facts about bivocational pastors during our formative years. Many of our members and pastors will likely be able to recall that the apostle Paul was a "tentmaker" as well as a pastor, evangelist and church planter. Some church history aficionados in our ranks would also know that some of our early church fathers were bivocational ministers: Chrysostom, a farmer-pastor; Spyridon, bishop of Cyprus, a shepherd-pastor; Dionysius, a physician-pastor; and that Benedict of Nursia required all the monks of the Benedictine order, including himself, to be occupied with manual labor in order to financially support themselves. But very few members—or even pastors

---

[10] Dorr, 21.

[11] Kennon L. Callahan, *Small, Strong Congregations: Creating Strengths and Health for Your Congregation* (San Francisco, CA: Jossey-Bass, 2000), 13.

in the RCA—will be able to tell you that the very first ministers in the RCA were bivocational pastors and that many of our most recognized pastors from the early years of our denomination were also bivocational pastors.

Jan Huyck and Bastian Krol, the first two men who were sent to the United States in the 1620s by the Dutch West India Company to provide pastoral care to the early settlers in regions now known as New York City and Albany in New York, also maintained other vocations while performing pastoral duties. These men, called "comforters of the sick," were not ordained ministers but were nonetheless charged with conducting worship, leading prayer services, catechizing the young, and visiting the sick.[12] These duties were later expanded to include performing marriages and baptisms.[13] They were not permitted to celebrate the Lord's Supper or preach sermons on their own, but by reading approved sermons and following the prescribed liturgy of the Reformed Church in the Netherlands, these men effectively pastored these colonial communities. At the same time, Jan Huyck was a storekeeper for the Dutch West India Company,[14] Bastian

---

[12] Howard Hageman, *Lily Among the Thorns* (New York: Half Moon Press, 1953), 57.

[13] Gerald F. De Jong, *The Dutch Reformed Church in the American Colonies* (Grand Rapids, MI: Eerdmans, 1978), 13.

[14] Arie R. Brouwer, *Reformed Church Roots* (Grand Rapids, MI: Eerdmans, 1977), 33.

Krol was an agent of the Dutch West India Company,[15]and it is believed that both continued in these dual-roles even after the first ordained minister arrived in 1628.[16]

Many of our early ordained ministers struggled financially to serve our churches. Although they were paid by the Dutch West India Company the same wage as their colleagues in the Netherlands, the cost of living was four times higher in the American colonies.[17] This made it extremely difficult for a pastor to support a family. So it was not unusual, then, to find these early ministers in the Reformed Church in America pursuing an additional trade, often as a farmer or a schoolteacher. Jonas Michaelius, the first ordained minister in the RCA, worked a farm to make ends meet.[18] Johannes Megapolensis, who served in a two church pastorate in the Netherlands before becoming the first pastor of the Fort Orange congregation in Albany, New York, was also expected to provide "duties and favors" for the local governor (called a "patroon") as well as the pastoral needs for his congregation.[19] Gideon Schatts was called to pastor churches in Albany and Rensselaer while also supplementing his "wages" as

---

[15] De Jong, 13.
[16] De Jong, 14.
[17] De Jong, 22.
[18] De Jong, 27.
[19] De Jong, 22.

the village schoolmaster.[20] These famous early ministers in the RCA were, by definition, bivocational pastors.

Notice, Schatts was called to pastor two churches at the same time. This is also, by definition, a regular form of bivocational ministry. Not surprisingly, we find this a common practice in the early days of the colonial church where both the villages and the churches were often small. Johannes Casparus Freyenmoet was called to pastor churches in Kinderhook, Claverack, and Livingston Manor, New York.[21] Laurentius Van Gaasbeek was the pastor of congregations in Kingston, Hurley, and Marbletown, New York.[22] David Marinus received a call extended by the congregations of Passaic, Pompton Plains, and Paterson, New Jersey.[23] Even the prominent Theodorus Jacobus Frelinghuysen, often credited with sparking "The Great Awakening" in America along with William Tennent, Jonathan Edwards, and George Whitefield,[24] received his call to come to America by agreeing to serve a pastorate consisting of four churches in the Raritan Valley of New Jersey.[25]

In 1664, when the English gained control over the

---

[20] De Jong, 25.

[21] De Jong, 115.

[22] De Jong, 67.

[23] De Jong, 115.

[24] William Dayton Brown, *History of the Reformed Church in America* (New York: Board of Publication and Bible School Work, 1928), 59.

[25] De Jong, 173-174.

territory formerly held by the Dutch, the Dutch West India Company withdrew its financial support of the pastors. And, as one historian writes, "The people were not accustomed to making contributions in sufficient amounts to pay salaries and support the church, and the ministers found themselves without funds with which to provide their daily bread."[26] Some went door to door asking their members for regular contributions; others like Samuel Megapolensis, son of Johannes Megapolensis, decided this was too degrading and returned to the Netherlands; still more like Gideon Schaats wanted to leave but were said to be too poor to go anywhere.[27]

The trend of RCA pastors supplementing the incomes furnished by their congregations continued throughout the years. Some congregations, acknowledging this need, tried to help their pastor find revenues outside the church, even providing lands for the pastor to farm or rent out. One call sent to the Netherlands in 1730 seeking a pastor for the churches in Freehold and Middletown, New Jersey, promised the pastor a seventy pound salary per year, a suitable parsonage, the use of one hundred acres of land, and a good riding horse. If the pastor lacked the skill to farm the land himself, the call stipulated that he could rent the land out to someone else for one-third of its yield.[28]

In this way, the RCA churches were little different

---

[26] Brown, 38-39.

[27] Brown, 39.

[28] De Jong, 118.

from other Protestant denominations in the United States. Throughout our history, many of our congregations were small gatherings of believers who struggled to receive the ministry of ordained pastors or to provide for their needs. Most churches "shared" a pastor with other congregations or were served by a pastor who supplemented their income by farming, teaching, or some other occupation. The same was true for Methodist churches, Presbyterian churches, Southern Baptist churches, and many others. Often these churches were led by strong, spiritual lay people who cared for the congregation and community in the absence of an ordained minister, or when the pastor they shared with another congregation was scheduled to preach at the other church (or churches) they served that Sunday. At times, an ordained minister was only leading worship and preaching at a particular church one Sunday per month and, in some instances, just once per quarter for the administration of the sacraments.

And yet, these congregations not only survived, but many of them are still serving and glorifying God today. My church is one of them. Perhaps, your church is one as well. In any case, we can be sure of this: We are both here today because of them; because God was at work in these often small, struggling congregations; because the gospel they cherished and shared has come to us down through the generations; and because a church of any size, as they live in faith and hope, matters to God.

OUR PRESENT CHALLENGE

This is as true today as it was throughout church history. I don't believe it is a secret that more and more of our churches in the United States are becoming smaller churches. As you know, there are many reasons for this. A church can decline because of a local factory closing or a change in population, because of church conflict or poor leadership, and because of a growing secularized culture or the failure of a church to preach the gospel. These are just a few examples. It is also the case that some of our churches have always been small.

And let's not forget that quite a few of our churches have not changed in size—they were averaging 75 souls in worship for the past 30 years—but now they can no longer afford to pay a full-time pastor. These churches may not have changed in size, but they have certainly changed the way the life and ministry of their church is carried out. Even more significantly, these churches, like many other smaller churches, may now perceive themselves very differently: As less competent, or less important, or less valuable in the kingdom of God simply because they no longer have a "full-time" minister.

They are not the only ones. In his book, *The Work of the Bivocational Pastor*, Dennis Bickers tells about a conversation that he overheard while in a Christian bookstore between two recent seminary graduates, one of whom worked in the store. They were discussing their ongoing search for a church to serve in as new pastors and were expressing their frustrations in what calls were being offered to them. One of these men stated that the only calls he was receiving came from a few small churches in rural areas. He then declared, quite dismissively, that he wasn't going to "waste his time" with those little churches.[29]

Attitudes like this toward smaller churches are not uncommon. Many people, clergy and laity alike, have a notion that smaller churches are inferior to larger churches; are less healthy and more difficult to lead than more substantial churches; and that they have failed, or are failing, to provide for the spiritual needs of their members and communities. As David Ray has said, himself a small church pastor, "To many, small means failure, inadequacy, immaturity, or a stage that precedes legitimacy."[30]

These views, unfortunately, are often held by smaller churches about themselves. Dennis Bickers insists that many small churches have serious struggles in how positively they should view themselves.[31] David Ray agrees. "The largest problem facing smaller churches," he writes, "is not a shortage of people or money. Instead, the most dominating and debilitating problem is more often low moral, resulting in negative self-esteem."[32]

In the same way, many people have a low opinion of the

---

[29] Bickers, *The Work of the Bivocational Pastor*, 4.
[30] Ray, x.
[31] Bickers, *The Work of the Bivocational Pastor*, 5.
[32] Ray, 191.

pastors who serve in these smaller churches. After all, they may sometimes think, if they were any good, wouldn't they be in a bigger church, or have a more substantial ministry, or be offered a position in a church that would pay them more? This way of thinking is too often applied to part-time pastors. *Why can't he get a call to a full-time church? What's wrong with him? Why can't she move on and get a "real" pastoral call? What has she done that was so damaging to her career?*

I appreciate what Ray Gilder, a pastor to bivocational ministers, has to say about this. He reminds us that we often hold in high esteem missionaries who serve the Lord and live their lives in obscure places in foreign countries among small communities of people while, at the same time, we ignore or denigrate pastors who do the very same thing in our own country.[33] He has a point. I used to think this way. Since then, I have learned that small churches should be considered contemporary "mission fields" and the pastors who are called to serve in them need to be treated with the same respect and admiration that missionaries often receive from the wider church community.

At times, those who hold this low view of small church pastors, and part-time calls, are the pastors themselves.[34] We are sometimes prone to being affected by what others

---

[33] Ray Gilder, *Uniquely Bivocational: Understanding the Life of a Pastor Who Has a Second Job* (Forest, VA: Salt and Light Publishing, 2013), 9.
[34] Steve R. Bierly, *How to Thrive as a Small-Church Pastor: A Guide to Spiritual and Emotional Well-Being* (Grand Rapids, MI: Zondervan, 1998), 38-41.

think of us, and what others think of our churches. The result is that we are made to feel like second class citizens in the kingdom of God—along with our churches—as we are compared to full-time pastors and their larger congregations.[35] This is not a good mindset for ministry. Nor is it likely to produce any long-tenured pastorates.

Sadly, this perception makes finding ministers to serve in small churches or to accept a call to a part-time pastorate increasingly difficult. Some think that it is hard to fill an empty pulpit in a small church because there is a shortage of ministers. A recent study has concluded that this is not the case. There is no shortage of ministers; there is, instead, an increasing number of ministers who are reluctant to serve in these ministries.[36] Truth be told, to many pastors, ministry in small churches has a bad reputation. It is not fair, but it is a reality that must be acknowledged. And let's face it: At times, there is some truth to it. If a church doesn't seem excited about ministry, or is resistant to change; if it lacks a vision for the future, or has a negative self-image simply because it is small or struggles to pay the bills, then it may not be an attractive call for any pastor.

For some churches, the simple fact of having a part-time pastor, or having to "downsize" to a part-time pastor, leads a church to a negative self-perception. After all, "real" churches have a full-time minister, don't they?

---

[35] Bickers, 57-58.

[36] Patricia M. Y. Chang, "Assessing the Clergy Supply in the 21st Century," *Pulpit and Pew: Research on Pastoral Leadership*, 2004.

They will often think that, if they can only build up their numbers and finances again to afford a full-time minister, then the church will be vital and healthy again. In some cases, yes, that may be true. Yet, let's not forget that many of our churches actually declined under the leadership of a full-time pastor. And many of our churches have been revived, have grown well and thrived, under the leadership of a part-time pastor. Maybe, having a full-time pastor versus having a part-time pastor is not a major key to church health, after all. Perhaps, the real key to church health, the person we should be looking for, is the *right* pastor for the church. What do you think?

I think that there is no reason for a congregation to feel bad about themselves simply because they are small in numbers, they do not have many resources, or don't have a full-time pastor. And pastors should not imagine that God thinks any less of them because they are serving in a small church, as a part-time pastor, and in a ministry that few people honor, admire, or esteem. Unless, of course, they have a good reason to.

Let's face it: Some churches and some pastors should feel bad about themselves. Some churches have abandoned the gospel, have been rife with conflict, are controlled by boorish leaders, do "chew-up-and-spit-out new pastors," or have been served by lazy or incompetent ministers. It does happen, right?

However, this is not true of *all* small churches. I do not believe it is anywhere near a majority of small churches.

Instead, let me go so far as to say that I believe the majority of small churches are faithful congregations genuinely committed to loving God and their neighbors.

This does not mean we are perfect. Sometimes, yes, we are not as eager to invite our friends and family to worship as we used to be. Sometimes, we are not as willing to talk about our faith with our neighbors as we should be. Sometimes, we are not as open to accommodating the way things are done in the church to the likes of others—unless they are big contributors to the church!—as we know Jesus would like us to be. And sometimes, yes, we resist change.

But know this: These behaviors are not confined to small churches. Congregations of 100, and 200, and even 300 also fall into these patterns. Larger churches are just as prone to settle in and get comfortable as smaller churches. However, please don't misunderstand what I am saying. I am not saying that this behavior is OK because "everyone is doing it." What I am saying is that no church is perfect, that smaller churches don't get "a pass" from fulfilling their God-given purpose just because they are small, and that every church has to work hard at being the church of Jesus Christ. This applies to the members and pastors alike.

Not every congregation—or pastor—knows what a "healthy" small church looks like. Many of us just "do church" the way we've been used to doing it for years without giving it much thought. *This must be what a church does,* we think; *after all, this is the way it has been done here for years!* Some of us are trained to think about our church, and the way our church is supposed to function, by those who have been around our church for a long time. For example, if we are a newly elected deacon, and if during our first few leadership meetings the discussions center on paying the bills and planning the next church supper, then we might form the impression that the leadership of the church is only called by the Lord to "manage" the church. On the other hand, if conversations are focused primarily on bringing communion to the shut-ins, how to enhance the experience of worship during the Sunday services, and ways to share the gospel with your community, we will likely come away with a much different idea about the role of leaders in your church—and a different view of the purpose of the church itself.

So, what does a "healthy" small church look like? I am convinced that a healthy small church has a positive self-image; they are not prone to equating size with significance in the eyes of God. They know the true mission of the church, derived from the Word of God, which gives their congregation a sense of unity and purpose. In all ways, they are devoted to following the teachings of the Bible. People are welcomed and enfolded into these churches, even as they continue to highly value family ties, heritage, and tradition. Their members understand the importance of faithful stewardship. Ministry is embraced as the calling of every Christian, not just the pastor. Leadership is based on spiritual maturity and giftedness, not on seniority or community status. And, above all, Jesus is proclaimed as their Lord and Savior, as true Head of the His church.[37]

The same could be said about the role of the pastor—that many people within the church do not really know what a pastor is supposed to be and do. Many of us assume we know what a pastor is supposed to be and do in the church—after all, some of us have been keeping watch on our pastors for years!—but do we really know what the Word of God reveals about this important ministry to His church? What about a part-time pastor? Is the ministry of a part-time pastor somehow different than a full-time pastor?

The answers to these questions seem obvious, but they are not. They are derived from our understanding of the nature and purpose of the church as well as our appreciation of who all of us are—pastors and members alike—as disciples of Jesus Christ and members of His church. For a small church to have a healthy and fruitful ministry with their part-time pastor, both the pastor and the congregation need to hear and follow what the Bible has to say about these things. We will turn our attention to these questions in the next chapter.

---

[37] See Bickers, *The Healthy Small Church*, 10.

OUR HOPE

The good news for small churches is that, with the right leadership, you can enjoy a strong, healthy and fruitful ministry. As long as your pastor—and you—have an understanding, heart, and vision for the small church, you are on the right path.

I am certain that the most critical factor necessary to having a healthy and fruitful ministry—for a part-time pastor *and* the church they serve with—is for both to know they have been called by God to this ministry for their time and place. Most people, I suspect, would agree with me that the pastor needs to appreciate a call from God to this particular ministry. But the church should also understand that they, along with their pastor, are called by God to this particular ministry at this time in their church's history.

This sense of divine calling will build up the church. It will guard against a negative self-image. And it will enable that church to respond to this form of ministry with hope and great anticipation that God is preparing to do something great and glorious through them. A congregation with this mindset will believe that they have something significant to offer the world in the name of Jesus Christ.[38]

Today, there are many small churches that are healthy and thriving in this way. And there are many pastors

---

[38] Bickers, *The Work of the Bivocational Minister*, 6-7.

serving in these churches who are gratified and grateful for their unique calling and are producing good fruit for the kingdom of God, fruit that will last. They see their churches as precious in the sight of God and capable of providing quality ministry in their community. Together with their congregations they are models of Christian faith and ministry. What does this look like? As Anthony Pappas has so well written:

> Leadership that seeks God's heart, leadership that loves the small church, leadership that understands the nature of the small church and can act appropriately within it. This type of leadership cares about the small church. It believes that each congregation is a magnificent creation of almighty God and that each congregation is called to a ministry that it alone can accomplish. It believes that each congregation, no matter how small, is a mission outpost in its time and place. And it believes that each congregation has its own wonder and beauty that by, believing in it, can be released.[39]

---

[39] Anthony G. Pappas, *Entering the World of the Small Church* (Bethesda, MD.: Alban Institute, 2000), 9.

QUESTIONS FOR REFLECTION

1. *Does knowing that churches have mostly been led by part-time pastors throughout church history change your understanding—or opinion—of part-time pastors?*

2. *How many churches in your area, or classis, are serves by part-time pastors?*

3. *How high or low a view do you hold for part-time pastors? Can you say why?*

4. *Why do you think small churches often have a negative self-image?*

5. *What does a healthy small church look like to you?*

Chapter 2
OUR SHARED CALLING

One thing is absolutely clear in the Word of God: All Christians are called to full-time ministry. All Christians are called to bear fruit as disciples of Jesus Christ (Jn 15:5-8). Jesus insists, "You did not choose me, but I chose you and appointed you that you should go and bear fruit" (Jn 15:16).

This is the case of every believer regardless of what your work is. If you are a believer—and if you work as a butcher, a baker, or a candlestick maker—you are "called" into full-time Christian ministry. The manner in which we carry out our calling will be unique to our gifts, passions, professions, locations, and even our personalities, but we all share the same experience of being "called" by God.

This must be kept in mind as we explore the call of a pastor to a "part-time" church. As a believer, a pastor in a "part-time" church is already called to a full-time ministry, just like every other Christian. Even when a pastor is working as a registered nurse on the night shift or driving a bus on weekday mornings, they remain always in full-time ministry. "Whatever you do, in word and deed," we are commanded, "do everything in the name of the Lord Jesus" (Col 3:17).

Remember, the apostle Paul was working as a tent-maker while engaged in pastoral ministry. Is it appropriate to say that he only served the Lord or His people part-time? Not really. When God calls a person, His call engages a person's whole being in service to the Lord. Our whole being means: who we are and what we do; all our time and all our life. Jesus said, "You shall love the Lord your God with all your heart and with all your soul and with all your mind," and "love your neighbor as yourself" (Mt 22:37-39).

Are you ready to do some practical theology? Let's first take a closer look at what it means to be "called" a Christian.

The Calling of a Christian

This calling, as Os Guiness defines it, "is the truth that God calls us to himself so decisively that everything we are, everything we do, and everything we have is invested with a special devotion, dynamism, and direction lived out as a response to his summons and service."[40] Simply stated: *We are called to be Christians, first and foremost, and this reality influences every aspect of our lives.*

---

[40] Guiness, 4.

This is our life's primary calling, or vocation, from which every other "calling" we receive in our life is derived and depends. By God's grace, this includes a call to relationship with God through Jesus Christ, a call to a new way of life in Christ involving our character and conduct, and a call to Christian service which God has prepared especially for us (Eph 2:8-10).[41] As you can see, the first calling we receive is a *calling to salvation*. Essentially, we are called *to* God. This is what makes us a believer in the first place—a person who knows and has been saved by God—and who is now "called" a child of God.[42]

What follows this call *to* God is a call to live *like* God, in true righteousness and holiness (Eph 4:24). "Be imitators of God, the apostle Paul explains, "as beloved children" (Eph 5:1). All the moral instruction in the Bible unfolds what this looks like in a believer's life, but the true portrait of the Christian life is found most fully in Jesus Christ, in both his teaching and his life. We are called to live through Jesus (Gal 2:20), by the power of the Holy Spirit (Acts 1:8; Gal 5:25), that we would be holy and blameless before God (Eph 1:4), maturing into the likeness of Christ (Rom 8:29). One can say that our primary

---

[41] Derek J. Prime and Alistair Begg, *On Being a Pastor: Understanding Our Calling and Work* (Chicago, IL: Moody, 2004), 19-20. I am indebted to these pastors for this three-fold understanding of God's call, which I will build upon below.

[42] Edmond P. Clowney, *Called to Ministry* (Phillipsburg, NJ: P&R, 1964), 10.

vocation to be a Christian also contains a calling to be *like* Christ. This is our second calling, which I refer to as our *calling to sanctification.*

When we understand these first two callings can we then appreciate the next calling, the calling to ministry, which is bound to and flows from the previous ones. In my mind, they form the "trinity" of our Christian vocation; there is not one without the others. Even as we are called *to* God, and called to be *like* God, we are also called *for* God. This is our third calling, which I refer to as our *calling to service.*

These callings to salvation, sanctification, and service are simply three aspects of our Christian vocation. It is appropriate to talk of three distinct "callings" as part of a single call to Christian vocation because these three callings are often heard at different times in a believer's life. As we mature in the life of faith, as we receive and apply Word and Sacrament to our lives, as we participate in the worship and fellowship and mission of the church, our calling to sanctification and our own calling to service will be heard.

Since, then, all Christians are called to a life of service, a life *for* God, a life of full-time ministry, what form of work or activities should this be? What about a bivocational pastors? Are only full-time pastors properly living out their Christian vocation?

The Calling of a Part-Time Pastor

Certainly, it must be said, that full-time pastors are fulfilling their calling to *service* as an aspect of their Christian vocation. Derek Prime and Alistair Begg, two long-time pastors, define the calling to pastoral ministry as "the unmistakable conviction an individual possesses that God wants him to do a specific task."[43] As a pastor, I like the sound of that. And I wholeheartedly agree. But this statement also requires a follow-up question: How much of a person's life is to be occupied with the "specific task" of pastoral ministry? In other words, if we agree what the "specific task" of pastoral ministry is, does that leave room for anything else?

This is a question about the whole life of a Christian pastor. It involves not only the roles and duties one carries out as a pastor of a church—preaching and teaching, and so forth—but also includes everything else a pastor does and everyone else a pastor sees, whether it is in the church, in the home, in the grocery store, on the golf course, or out on the street. All of these are places and people to be touched by a pastor's ministry, for all of these belong to God (Ps 24:1).

This means, as I will insist again, that there is never a time that a pastor is not "the pastor" of the church. Many hour a week are spent within the walls of the church

---

[43] Prime and Begg, 18.

building, or in the homes of church families, or in the hospital with church members and friends, but there are other hours that occupy the pastor's week that are "outside" the church. In either case, one does not stop being the pastor of the church. This is as true for part-time pastors as it is for full-time pastors. As a part-time pastor, I remain the pastor while I am having dinner with my family, when I am sitting in the service station waiting for an oil change on my car, and even when I am on a two-week vacation in Maine. This is so even when I am working as a registered nurse, what many in my church call my "other job."

The truth is: Pastoral ministry is never a part-time calling. As Dennis Bickers has stated about his own duties as a bivocational pastor:

> I had the same number of sermons to prepare as pastors of much larger churches. (In fact, I may have had more sermons to prepare because I didn't have people on staff to preach for me.) My members went into the hospital and expected pastoral visits. Church members and others in the community called upon me to conduct their weddings and officiate at their funerals. Like many pastors, I was on call 24/7, and I was excited to be involved in the lives of our congregation.[44]

---

[44] Bickers, *The Work of the Bivocational Pastor*, 3.

It is clear, then, there is no difference in the calling of a part-time pastor compared to a full-time pastor. In fact, the only real distinction—which does not change the nature of the calling itself—is the actual number of hours per week that one is contracted to perform the duties of a pastor within the church. Some bivocational pastors see the work they do outside the church as work they do *for* the church— as if they are still working for the church—since this "other job" actually allows them to serve in a church that can't afford to fully pay them otherwise. In any event, we remain in full-time ministry no matter where we are, what we are doing, or who we are with. And as we will see, it doesn't change the "specific task" of pastoral ministry either.

This is simply a pastor's response to the call of God on his or her life. It is one aspect of our Christian vocation— along with being a spouse, a parent, a friend, a neighbor, and the like. And it is just as personal and just as sacred as a Christian answering a call of God to be a nurse, a mechanic, a teacher, or a mother, as they live the whole of their life *for* God and His glory. As Martin Luther has said, "The works of monks and priests, however holy and arduous they be, do not differ one whit in the sight of God from the works of the rustic laborer in the field or the woman going about her household tasks, but that all works are measured before God by faith alone."[45]

---

[45] Martin Luther, *The Babylonian Captivity of the Church* (n.p.: FigBooks, 2012), 3.42, Kindle.

This being said, a person can be called by God to be a nurse or a pastor, a farmer or a pastor, a mother or a pastor—or even both, a nurse *and* a pastor—in our calling to service for the Lord. The essential trait of every Christian ministry, for the pastor or the homemaker alike, is simply this: "Whatever you do, in word and deed, do everything in the name of the Lord Jesus, giving thanks to God the Father through him" (Col 3:17).

THE PRIESTHOOD OF ALL BELIEVERS

Remember, the pastor is not the only "minister" in the church. The term "to minister" simply means "to serve." For this reason, John Stott, in *Basic Christianity*, asserts, "God calls every Christian to ministry, that is, to service, to be the servant of other people for the sake of Christ."[46] This calling to service is received and clarified within the church. Even more, this calling to service is to take place both within the church—for the sake of others in the church—and within the world, as we reach out personally and with the community of faith to impact the world for Christ.

The role of the church in our spiritual life and development cannot be overstated. John Calvin went so far as to insist that, as God is our Father, so the church is our Mother. In the *Institutes of Christian Religion*, he writes,

---

[46] John R. W. Stott, *Basic Christianity* (Grand Rapids, MI, Eerdmans, 1998), 113.

Let us learn, from her single title of Mother,
how useful, no, how necessary the knowledge of her is, since there is no other means
of entering into life unless she conceive us
in her womb and give us birth, unless she
nourish us at her breasts and, in short, keeps
us under her charge and government, until,
divested of mortal flesh, we become like the
angels (Mt 22:30). For our weakness does
not permit us to leave her school until we
have spent our whole lives as scholars.[47]

This is a fitting image, don't you think? Since our life
of faith begins through the church as we hear and respond
to the gospel preserved and proclaimed by the church; as
we continue to grow and gain spiritual health through
the care, encouragement, love, teaching, and correction
we receive from the church; and as we head out into the
world to live a life of holiness and service, we will always
need the guidance, support, and prayers of the church. It is
a vital *relationship* that sustains us our entire Christian life.

This means, of course, that every Christian has a vital
role to play in the church for the sake of others. To say we
need the church to find life and growth in the Christian
faith is simply to say that we need one another, since

[47] John Calvin, *Institutes of the Christian Religion*, trans. Henry Beveridge
(Peabody, MA: Hendrickson, 2008), 674.

together we are the church. "Once we understand discipleship in the broader sense of helping one another live our Christian lives," pastor Stephen Smallman has said, "then the absolute necessity of the church community comes to the foreground."[48] I am to look for instruction and care *from* other members of the church even I am to offer love and guidance *to* other members of the church. This is precisely what we hear in the Word of God. We are to "care for" one another (1 Cor 12:25), "encourage" one another (1 Thes 5:11), "admonish" one another (1 Thes 5:14), "love" one another (Jn 13:34), "pray" for one another (Jas 5:16), and the like. Bottom line: We are to be ministers to one another inside the church even as we serve as ministers to those outside the church.

This is what believers in many traditions refer to as the "priesthood of all believers." Hear how this is described in *Reformed: What It Means, Why It Matters*: "All believers share in the special calling of being Christ's representatives on earth. We do that in different ways. Clergy, priests and ministers do it one way. Factory workers, nurses, and lawyers do it in other ways. But we all devote our life and our life's work to God's service. That makes all of us priests."[49] In 1 Peter 2:5 we hear, "You, yourselves, like living stones are being built up as a spiritual house, to be a holy priesthood, to offer spiritual sacrifices acceptable

---

[48] Smallman, 21.

[49] Robert De Moor, *Reformed: What It Means, Why It Matters* (Grand Rapids, MI: Faith Alive, 2009), 45.

to God through Jesus Christ." Thus, the priesthood of all believers is an essential way of understanding our calling to service in the Christian life.

As you can hear, this means that the ministry of the church has not been entrusted solely to the hands of the ordained or "professional" Christians, as if the rest of the congregation has nothing to do but passively sit by to receive the ministry of the clergy. The meaning of the "priesthood of all believers" is that all Christians serve in ministry *together* and that the work of the church is a shared responsibility and a mutual necessity.

This reminder that all Christians are included in the priesthood of the church serves the church as a healthy corrective, assuring us that there is no separation between the clergy and laity in the call to ministry. We are all believers. We all belong to Christ. Therefore, we are all His ministers. We simply fill different roles.

This is why, in 1 Corinthians 12, the apostle Paul speaks about the different spiritual gifts that have been given to each individual person in the church. "Now there are a variety of gifts, but the same Spirit; and there are varieties of service, but the same Lord; and there are varieties of activities, but it is the same God who empowers them in everyone. To each is given a manifestation of the Spirit for the common good" (1 Cor 12:4-7). The apostle Peter also calls upon the church, as individual believers, to view our personal gifts as for the common good. "As each has received a gift," he says, "use it to serve one another, as good stewards of God's varied grace" (1 Pt 4:10).

What is clear in Scripture is that there are a variety of ways that Christians are called to acts of service, and that each one of us contributing our part is essential, not only to the health and purpose of the individual, but also to the vitality and work of the church as a whole. Comparing the church to a physical body, the Bible goes on to say in 1 Corinthians 12,

> For the body does not consist in one member but many. If the foot should say, 'Because I am not a hand, I do not belong to the body,' that would not make it any less a part of the body...The eyes cannot say to the hand, 'I have no need of you," nor the head to the feet, 'I have no need of you,'...But God so composed the body, giving greater honor to the part that lacked it, that there be no division in the body, but that the members may have the same care for one another. (12:14-25).

If this is true for any local congregation, then consider how much more it is true for a smaller congregation that may have only one pastor—or only one part-time pastor. Because if the church is relying on *only* the pastor to carry out the mission of the church, then that church is seriously weak, not to mention much less effective, then when all the Christians in the congregation are actively involved in ministry.

Furthermore, as the Bible demonstrates, no one person receives all the gifts for the church. They are distributed among all the members as the Holy Spirit sees fit. This means that no one person—not even the pastor—is able to carry out the work of the church all on their own. And to try to do so, without enlisting the gifts and responsibilities of others, would actually impede or even *rob* other church members of the essential work that God desires then to do as ministers in the church of Christ.

This does not mean, of course, that we are all ministers in the same way. There is a division of roles prescribed in the Scriptures. These roles enable us to support and care for one another in our assigned ministries. Every member and every gift is needed for the church, but we also need some faithful and mature leaders to teach, guide, and care for us as we serve.

All Christians are ministers; but not all Christians are pastors.[50] And we are not all called to be leaders, at least not at first. We may first need a season of preparation and instruction in the faith; a certain time to grow in doctrine and wisdom, to increase in knowledge and humility, to gain in truth and love; and we will need op-

---

[50] Michael Horton, *The Christian Faith: A Systematic Theology for Pilgrims On the Way* (Grand Rapids, MI: Zondervan, 2011), 882.

portunities to test and confirm our gifts and callings. In fact, all Christians need these things. For this we need the church. We need the church to help us become faithful and obedient disciples of Jesus Christ. This is the role of all our leaders in the church, including elders and deacons, along with the pastor.

In the Reformed tradition (as in others), our leaders in the church are men and women "called by God, gifted by the Holy Spirit, and elected by the church to fulfill leadership functions in the church essential to the life and witness of the whole."[51] This is the function of not only the pastors, but of elders and deacons as well, who make up the consistory (governing body) of the local church. They all share the work of leading and governing the church.

Now, let me state this as directly as I can. Fulfilling their vital tasks in ministry as elders and deacons in the church—as outlined in the Bible—is as crucial to the health and mission of the church as the pastor fulfilling his or her duties. As far as I know, every church in my denomination has elders and deacons serving on their consistory. But not every church in my denomination has elders and deacons actually living out their calling as elders and deacons as given by God.

The consistory is not a "board of directors" elected to administer policies, to manage programs, to pay the bills,

---

[51] Robert White, *The Ministry of the Elder* (New York: Reformed Church Press, 1996), 4.

to care for the property, or to direct and evaluate the pastor in the performance of his or her duties. To be sure, they do these things—and need to do these things—but if this is all that they do, the church is impoverished because of it. Elders and deacons, as fellow ministers, are to personally join with the pastor in caring for the spiritual life and health of the church and community. I am convinced that a church cannot be healthy and grow, spiritually or otherwise, without all the leadership of the church—pastors, elders, and deacons—fulfilling their own God-given calling in the church.

The office of elder is particularly responsible for the spiritual oversight of the congregation.[52] According to the *Book of Church Order of the Reformed Church in America*, elders are "set apart for a ministry of watchful and responsible care for all matters relating to the welfare and good order of the church. They are to study God's Word, to oversee the household of faith, to encourage spiritual growth, to maintain loving discipline, and to provide for the proclamation of the gospel and the celebration of the sacraments."[53] This ministry includes oversight of all other officers in the church, including the care of the pastor; assisting the pastor with good counsel; and even assisting the pastor in the visitation of all members and inquirers.[54]

---

[52] White, 10.

[53] Reformed Church in America, *Book of Church Order of the Reformed Church in America* (2012), 12.

[54] *Book of Church Order*, 12

The ministry of elders is complemented by the ministry of deacons. If pastors and elders are to be effective in their calling to service in their respective offices, concentrating their time and efforts on the spiritual life and health of their church and community, then the ministry of deacons is just as necessary and significant. In the book of Acts, in order to allow the apostles to devote themselves "to prayer and the ministry of the Word" (6:4), others were appointed to a ministry of service to those in need. Following this tradition, deacons are servants, called by God, entrusted with a ministry of "mercy, service, and outreach" both within the church and out into the world.[55] Deacons are especially called to lead others in the church to pursue acts and ministry of care in Jesus' name.[56]

One thing is clear: Ministry is not carried out by the pastor alone. This can never be the case because there is simply too much work to do. I agree with Robert LaRochelle who in his book, *Part-Time Pastor, Full-Time Church*, insists that there is no such thing as a "part-time" church even as there is no such thing as a part-time pastor. "The community of the church," he rightly states, "is a full-time reality."[57] As long as there are people who need to hear the gospel in our little neck of the woods, members

---

[55] Betty Voskuil, *The Ministry of the Deacon* (New York: Reformed Church Press, 2003), 2.

[56] Voskuil, 3-4.

[57] Robert LaRochelle, *Part-Time Pastor, Full-Time Church* (Cleveland, OH: Pilgrim Press, 2010), 14.

who need to grow in faith and love in the Lord, neighbors who need our help and compassion, children who need to know the love of God, seniors who need a visit or assistance, a world that needs our prayers and witness...you get the idea. There is plenty of ministry to be done.

To this end, the pastor, along with everyone else, has been called to a particular role within the priesthood of all believers. It is to the work of the church and the work part-time pastor we turn next.

QUESTIONS FOR REFLECTION

1. *Are all Christians called to full-time ministry? If this is true, in what way?*

2. *Can pastoral ministry ever be a part-time calling? Why or why not?*

3. *What is the meaning of the phrase "the priesthood of all believers"?*

4. *How significant is the role of elders and deacons in the church?*

5. *Are all churches "full-time" churches? Explain why or why not?*

Part Two:

THE WORLD OF THE PART-TIME CHURCH

Chapter 3

THE WORK OF THE CHURCH

A calling to ministry, for all Christians—pastors and congregation alike—is a call to service within a local church. In the New Testament, the word *ekklesia* means "to call out."[58] Jesus was the first to use the word *ekklesia* to refer to the church, applying it to the company of believers gathered around him who publically confessed that Jesus is Lord (Mt 16:18).[59] At its most essential level, you can say that this is who we are as Christians: those who, by the grace of God, have been chosen in Christ through the Holy Spirit to profess faith in Jesus Christ as our Lord and Savior.

A pastor and seminary professor named Edmond Clowney once called this the *Great Constitution* of the church.[60] In other words, if someone were to ask you,

---

[58] Louis Berkhof, *Systematic Theology* (Carlisle, PA: Banner of Truth Trust, 1958), 556.

[59] Berkhof, 556.

[60] Edmund J. Clowney, *The Church* (Downer's Grove, IL: InterVarsity, 1995), 160.

"What is the church?" the simplest, most basic answer you could give is to say: "The church is a gathering of people who profess that Jesus is their Lord and Savior." This constitutes who we are.

The Bible uses many images to represent the church, and they each contribute to providing a beautiful and hopeful picture of what this church of professing Christians is called to be. We are the children of God (Eph 5:1), the body of Christ (1 Cor 12:27), and the temple of the Holy Spirit (1 Cor 3:16), to name a few. In fact, these are dozens of images of the church in the Bible that inform us and inspire us to be the magnificent church that God desires us to be. And they all to various degrees stress our vital relationship to the person and work of Jesus Christ.

THE HEAD OF THE CHURCH

This is so, because the church belongs to Jesus. Christ founded the church and gave us our identity (Mt 16:18), He paid for us with His blood (Acts 20:28), and personally identifies Himself with His church (Acts 9:4). He is the true "head" of the body, the church and our life and ministry flow from Him alone (Eph 1:22; Col 1:18); as such, Jesus has full authority over the work of the church.

This is to say: *Jesus is the true leader of every local church.* Saying this, allow me to linger here a moment. Because this should be encouraging news for every congregation presently without a pastor, every church that is looking to call a new pastor, and every community of faith whose pastor is "at the other job." Jesus is always leading the church. He is leading your congregation right now. You are always on His mind. You are never left on our own. Even when you do have a pastor, Jesus is still the one in charge. The church belongs to Christ alone.

This means that Christ alone has the right to establish the mission of His church. Not the pastor. Not the elders. Not the members. Not the community. Only Christ. This is extremely important in any discussion about the mission of the church—the work we in a local church are directed to do by Christ. There are many competing voices, both within and outside the church, insisting that the church must get involved in any number of good causes (homelessness), community services (food pantry), and global needs (human trafficking). In other words, there are many people with many different ideas about what the church should be doing.

In response to this confusion, pastors Kevin DeYoung and Greg Gilbert offer a helpful path forward in their book, *What Is the Mission of the Church?*:

> At its most basic, the term *mission* implies two things to most people: (1) being sent and (2) being given a task. The first point makes sense because *mission* comes from a Latin word (*mittere*) meaning "to send." The second point is implied in the first. When

sent on a mission, we are sent to *do something*—and not *everything*, either, but rather
we are given a particular assignment...Even
in the world around us, everyone under-
stands that a mission is that primary thing
that you are sent out to accomplish.[61]

These pastors make a distinction between the essential
"mission" of the local *church* on one hand, and the various "good works" we may do as individual *Christians* on
the other. They acknowledge that there are many things
we as Christians are commanded by God to do in Jesus'
name this world, but that is not necessarily the work of the
church as a whole.[62] The work of the church, they insist,
is much narrower and more focused than what is expected
of individual Christians.[63]

Smaller churches need to understand this distinction.
So do part-time pastors. We as a church are not expected
to do every good work that is needed in our world, or is
asked of us by others. The local *church* and the individual
Christian have different work to do, although they certainly support and complement each other. As individual
Christians, we may set out in ministry in any number of

[61] Kevin DeYoung and Greg Gilbert, *What Is the Mission of the Church?:
Making Sense of Social Justice, Shalom, and the Great Commission* (Wheaton,
IL: Crossway, 2011), 19.

[62] DeYoung and Gilbert, 29.

[63] DeYoung and Gilbert, 233.

ways and settings according to our own personal call to service (working at a homeless shelter, volunteering with Meals-On-Wheels, supporting a local food pantry, etc.) but as a local church, our calling is more precise. And as we will see, when the local church fulfills its own mission, then we as individual Christians are greatly built up and better equipped to accomplish the good works we believe Jesus is calling each of us to personally pursue as disciples of Jesus Christ.

This is not to say that churches are to ignore people in need. Churches should be calling upon their members to serve in their communities and in this world as God directs them. They should be identifying and challenging areas of injustice, abuse and oppression wherever these are found. Even more, local churches—even joining with other churches—should be engaged in activities that meet the physical and social needs of others in loving and compassionate ways in the name of Jesus (Micah 6:8; Gal 2:10; James 1:27). As we have the opportunity, we are to "do good to everyone" (Gal 6:10). But these activities should never crowd out the other gospel ministries of the church. We are, after all, not a social service agency. We are the church of Jesus Christ and, as such, we have a different purpose than they do.

Bottom line: It is a question of keeping our priorities in order. Especially as a small church, a major factor regarding our involvement in helping ministries is the fact that our small church's resources are not unlimited, in either money or people. We cannot be all things for all people. This is paramount for a church with a part-time pastor. We have to make critical budget decisions, including how much we can pay our pastor, whether we can offer health coverage, what church programs and ministries we can finance, and how much financial support we can provide missionaries and to pressing local needs.

In addition, with limited resources in terms of people as well as money, how much time and effort we can expend on serving the physical and social needs of our community will impact what can be directed toward meeting the pastoral and spiritual needs of both the congregation and the community. Serving in a soup kitchen or a food pantry is important, essential, God-honoring service; no question about it. But so is coming together in worship, visiting the sick, hosting a Bible study in our home, and sharing the gospel of salvation with our neighbors. Knowing precisely what the church has been established to accomplish in the name of Jesus Christ, and keeping that purpose front and center in the life of the church, will help local church leaders and congregations make biblically discerning choices for the glory of God.

In the same way, this may also allow the bivocational pastor to prioritize his or her ministry in that church. When this happens, no doubt, both the church and the pastor will find more joy and satisfaction in ministry—by not feeling pulled in every direction. Instead, they can know they are living and serving faithfully to their call to ministry.

MAKING DISCIPLES

This is so, because *making disciples* who profess that Jesus Christ is their Lord and Savior is at the heart of what the church is commanded to do by Christ. Jesus said, "All authority in heaven and on earth has been given to me. Go, therefore, and make disciples of all nations, baptizing them in the name of the Father and of the Son and of the Holy Spirit, teaching them to observe all that I have commanded you. And behold, I am with you always, to the end of the age" (Mt 28:18-20). The single command of this passage is this: *make disciples*. The three dependent words—*go, baptizing,* and *teaching*—simply describe the ongoing aspects of this process of making disciples. This process includes an intentional action (*go*) of helping people make a public profession of faith and becoming part of the church (*baptizing*) and nurturing them in the way of following Jesus as his disciples (*teaching*).[64]

This is our *Great Commission*, commonly recognized as a foundational passage for determining the mission of the church. This is a work, we should note, that Jesus, Himself, accomplishes through us. "When we consider that Jesus began with a statement of His authority and ended it with an absolute promise of His ongoing presence as this great work is undertaken," pastor Stephen Smallman reminds

---

[64] Stephen Smallman, *What Is Discipleship?* (Phillipsburg, NJ: P&R Publishing, 2011), 7.

us, "we can properly conclude that making disciples of the nations is a work that Jesus himself is doing through his church."[65]

Another passage often cited alongside this one to define the mission of the church is Matthew 22:37-40, often called the *Great Commandment.* "You shall love the Lord your God with all your heart and with all your soul and with all your mind. This is the great and first commandment. And the second is like it: You shall love your neighbor as yourself. On these two commandments depend all the Law and the Prophets."

Rick Warren, in his book *The Purpose-Driven Church*, combines the "Great Commandment" and the "Great Commission" to formulate what he calls the five purposes of the church: worship, ministry, evangelism, fellowship, and teaching.[66] Many other pastors and authors have stated the same priorities of ministry, sometimes using slightly different terms (and sometimes a slightly different number of tasks) to describe the very same activities that serve our mission to make disciples. John Stott, for example, offers these same "purposes" for the church's mission in his discussion of the early church, drawn from Acts 2:42-47. In *The Living Church*, he outlines the mission of the church by emphasizing four essential characteristics he gleans from this passage: We are called to be a *learning* church, a *caring*

---

[65] Smallman, 7.

[66] Rick Warren, *The Purpose-Driven Church* (Grand Rapids, MI: Zondervan, 19950, 102-103.

church, a *worshipping* church, and an *evangelizing* church.[67] He uses the term "caring" church to define his understanding of fellowship while his depiction of the "evangelizing" church also includes what others call outreach or mission.[68]

I suggest that the ongoing process of making disciples would include at least these four foundational tasks: worship, discipleship, fellowship, and evangelism.[69]

> *Worship (the up-reach of the gospel)* would include the weekly gathering of the church to ascribe worth to God, to be nurtured in our faith through Word and Sacrament, and to offer up prayers for ourselves, our community, and our world.

---

[67] John Stott, *The Living Church* (Downer's Grove, IL: IVP Books, 2007), 22-33.

[68] Stott, *The Living Church*, 25-26, 47-69.

[69] I prefer the term "evangelism" to describe the related tasks of evangelism and outreach, since I believe both these tasks must serve as a witness to the gospel—with deeds of ministry always accompanied by an opportunity to share the gospel of Jesus Christ. Another reason I like the term "evangelism" is to keep this activity in the forefront of the church. With all the other activities in the church, evangelism can easily be neglected, and even forgotten, especially when we use terms like "outreach" or "ministry" which can obscure what we are trying to accomplish—bringing people to a saving relationship with God through faith in Jesus Christ.

Discipleship (the down-reach of the gospel) in-cludes all the activities of the church that develop and grow our knowledge and com-mitment to the Lord for all ages, enabling us to better live a life of holiness and service, maturing into the likeness of Christ.

Fellowship (the in-reach of the gospel) describes the various caring ministries of the church, especially to one another in the body of Christ.

Evangelism (the out-reach of the gospel) encom-passes our deliberate and intentional witness to Christ, both in word and in deed.

This is the mission, the purpose, the cause, the reason for being—however we might like to say it—of the church of Jesus Christ. This is what our Lord tells us to do. And, as you can no doubt see, this can be accomplished by a congrega-tion of any size, large or small. I happen to agree with Rick Warren that nothing can revitalize a discouraged church faster than that church rediscovering its biblical purpose.[70] I have discovered, firsthand, that this is true for pastors, too.

Even more, embracing this mission can help a small church and their pastor channel their attention, creativity,

[70] Warren, 81.

and energy on the quality of their ministry without being side-tracked by many lesser things. For the small church, *quality* must precede *quantity*. In other words, concentrating on church depth often leads to church growth. Imagine putting our time and resources into providing *inspiring* worship, *joyful* discipleship, *authentic* fellowship, and *loving* evangelism. What kind of church would that be? I, for one, would expect that to be the kind of church that Jesus would be leading. Even more, that would be the kind of church I would certainly want to be a part of—and invite others to be a part of as well. How about you?

QUESTIONS FOR REFLECTION

1. *Can you give a simple, basic answer to the question: What is the church?" Give it try.*

2. *Who decides what the mission of your church is? What is this mission?*

3. *If worship is one aspect of the mission of your church, what are some others?*

4. *Does your church use the term "evangelism" to describe one aspect of the mission of your church? Why or why not?*

5. *Why is quality in ministry important, especially for small churches?*

Chapter 4
THE WORK OF A PART-TIME PASTOR

A pastor of a local church is called by God to a ministry of service. Specifically, pastors "are called to proclaim the gospel of Jesus Christ and to the ministry of the Word of God. In the local church the minister serves as pastor and teacher of the congregation to build up and equip the whole church for its ministry in the world."[71] As you can hear, the *role* of this ministry is that of "pastor and teacher" with the *purpose* "to build up and equip the whole church for its ministry in the world."

TO BUILD UP AND EQUIP THE CHURCH

We have seen that the mission of the church is to make disciples through worship, fellowship, discipleship, and evangelism. The minister, then, is called to "build up and equip the whole church" to accomplish this particular mission.

---

[71] *Book of Church Order*, 12.

This is the minister's own calling to service for the church. Like any other Christian, he or she may also have other places where they are called to serve outside the local church (home, community, denomination, even another occupation or a second church), but building up and equipping the local church "for its ministry in the world" is what the congregation they are called to serve should expect from their minister. This is the pastor's calling within the local church, exclusively.

This is what is revealed in Scripture. Ephesians 4:11 states that God gave the church "pastors and teachers" for this particular service. Although some may view "pastors and teachers" as simply two names for the same ministry, I agree with John Stott who suggests that every pastor must be a teacher of the Word of God, but not all teachers of the Word of God need to be a pastor, such as those who serve in Christian schools, colleges, and seminaries.[72] This being said, I must stress that "pastor" and "teacher" belong together in the ministry of the pastor in a local church since "the shepherding aspect of the ministry keeps us in touch with reality—with genuine issues and problems—as we teach the Word of God. To teach the Scriptures effectively we must apply them, and, with the Spirit's help, we can do this only as we are in touch with things as they really are in the lives of men and women."[73]

---

[72] John R. W. Scott, *The Message of Ephesians* (Downer's Grove, IL: InterVarsity Press, 1979), 165-166.

[73] Prime and Begg, 31-31.

Teaching the Word of God is certainly the work of a pastor (1 Tm 3:2)—and it surely builds up and equips the church for worship, discipleship, fellowship, and evangelism—yet it is not the only thing needed by the church to fulfill its mission. It is not the only thing the church should require from its minister. Above all, as Ephesians 4:11 reveals, the church also needs a "pastor."

Glenn Daman, in *Leading the Small Church*, insists that "nothing is more fundamental and critical to the health of the church" than clarifying the role of the pastor in the church.[74] Although this applies to any church of any size, Daman emphasizes this absolute necessity for smaller churches. As we have seen, many churches today are being pulled in many different directions concerning their true calling and mission. But pastors are just as vulnerable to diversion and distraction. Many pastors are being asked to spend time and energy on matters within the church that may be peripheral or even unrelated to their biblical role in the church, not to mention the many areas outside the church that the pastor may be invited or expected to fill a role, often from the church members themselves. I have seen that the typical church places more demands on their pastor than the Bible does. [75]

Whatever else may be asked of a pastor by their congregation (and community)—whether it is attending

---

[74] Glenn C. Daman, *Leading the Small Church: How to Develop a Transformational Ministry* (Grand Rapids, MI: Kregel, 2006), 17.
[75] See also: Gilder, 35.

Rotary Club meetings, presiding over meetings of the property committee, or offering prayers at the Veteran's Day parade, and the like—nothing should be allowed to replace, distort, compromise, or distract from this vital calling of the pastor. All the other so-called "duties" or expectations of a pastor can also be performed by some other office holder or member of a church. The pastor has something else that requires his or her time, energy, and attention as determined by God. Priorities must be established. Expectations must be realistic. Therefore, clarifying the role of the pastor in the church is essential for enjoying a successful part-time arrangement for both the pastor and the congregation.[76]

SHEPHERD

Stated plainly, a pastor is a "shepherd."[77] The term "pastor" is derived from the Latin word for "shepherd."[78] In the New Testament, as in Ephesians 4:11, the Greek noun *poimen*, meaning "shepherd," is commonly translated

---

[76] Stephen Norcross, "The Bivocational Option," in *Inside the Small Church,* ed. Anthony G. Pappas (Baltimore, MD:Alban Institute, 2002), 67.

[77] The term "shepherd" can also apply to elders and their role in the church, especially in the Reformed tradition, where pastor and elders often can have similar and overlapping roles: the pastor as a "teaching elder" and the other elders as "ruling elders." See: Timothy Z. Witmer, *The Shepherd Leader* (Phillipsburg, NJ: P&R Publishing, 2010).

[78] Witmer, 2.

into English as "pastor."[79] Additionally, the Greek verb *poiemeno*, meaning "to shepherd," appears in the New Testament to describe the work of a pastor (Acts 20:28; 1 Pt 5:2) while the Greek noun for "flock" is used for the church (Acts 20:28-29; 1 Pt 5:2-3).[80]

This means, of course, that a pastor serves as a "shepherd" to a local church who is his "flock." Yet it is necessary to note that the congregation is not primarily the shepherd's flock. Jesus said to Peter, "Feed my sheep" (Jn 21:17). He didn't say, "Feed *your* sheep." This demonstrates that a pastor is really an under-shepherd to Jesus, who is the true shepherd of the church.

This image of the pastor as shepherd is essential for understanding how we are to exercise godly leadership and care for the church today, since this imagery is first applied to God, himself, in the Scriptures. "The LORD is my shepherd," we hear in Psalm 23:1. Similarly, this shepherd imagery is used for earlier leaders of God's people who were appointed to nurture and protect Israel, as under-shepherds, serving directly under the authority of God (Ps 78:71; Jer 23:2, Ez 34:11). In the New Testament, Jesus is the "good shepherd" who provides for and protects God's flock (Jn 10:11-18). As leaders in the church today, pastors are to be "shepherds of God's flock" which are

---

[79] Richards, 560.

[80] Peter T. O'Brien, *The Letter to the Ephesians* (Grand Rapids, MI: Eerdmans, 1999), 299.

under our care (1 Pt 5:2), closely following the pattern of pastoral ministry set by Jesus.[81]

Several prominent models of this shepherding ministry have been proposed to outline the various areas that require the careful and ongoing attention of a pastor. Timothy Laniak proposes the areas of provision, protection, and guidance.[82] Donald MacNair employs the acronym "GOES" for guardian, overseer, example, and shepherd.[83] And Timothy Witmer prefers knowing, feeding, leading, and protecting for the essential areas of a shepherding ministry.[84] Each of these is certainly biblical, instructive, and practical in gaining a well-rounded picture of a pastor's shepherding tasks. For our purposes, I will propose a concentration on these vital areas: a shepherd must *heed, feed, lead,* and *need* in service to Christ for his sheep.[85]

---

[81] Peter T. O'Brien, 300.

[82] Timothy S. Laniak, *While Shepherds Watch Their Flock: Rediscovering Biblical Leadership* (Matthews, NC: Shepherd Leader Publications, 2007).

[83] Donald MacNair, *The Practices of a Healthy Church* (Phillipsburg, NJ: P&R Publications, 1999).

[84] Witmer, 102.

[85] The categories of *heed, feed,* and *lead* are not original to me, but their origin has been lost. It is possible that I picked them up at a ministry conference many years ago. To these I have added *need* for reasons we will see below.

HEED

Even before a pastor can do anything else, he or she has to *heed*, that is, they must listen to, pay attention to, and yield to God in service for others in the church. This occurs in several ways. First, a pastor must heed the calling of God. This means we respond to God's voice in our calling to a particular ministry, to a specific flock, in a chosen time and setting.

We also heed the Word of God by grounding our person, conduct, and ministry firmly in the Scriptures. A pastoral life is filled with study and prayer. There is little a pastor can offer a church—even as it is impossible to biblically feed and lead the church—if the pastor lacks knowledge, maturity, and godliness in his or her own life. Some would insist that a church's greatest need is their pastor's own personal pursuit of holiness.[86] The truth that we as pastors are first sons and daughters of God who live our lives in answer to the Lord's call to us should come before anything else; this should be the church's greatest expectation for us since our calling, character and personal relationship with the Lord are central to our ministry.

Additionally, a shepherd must heed the sheep and their environment. In other words, a pastor spends time to get to know their congregation. Jesus said, "I am the good shepherd. I know my own and my own know me" (Jn

---

[86] Prime and Begg, 35.

10:14). Getting to know, understand, and love the congregation and becoming familiar with their strengths and
weaknesses, their needs and gifts, their setting and culture,
their heritage and traditions enables a pastor to belong to
that fellowship of Christians and to rightly know how to
feed and lead them. As equally important, no more so than
in a smaller church, the congregation is also given the opportunity to get to know their pastor and, God willing, to
learn to love and trust their pastor to feed and lead them.

FEED

Another important aspect of shepherding a flock is to *feed*
them. Jesus said, "Feed my sheep" (Jn 21:16). Again, the
Word of God takes a prominent position here. Nothing takes
the place of sound biblical preaching and teaching in the life
and health of a church. This is especially the case for small
churches. When a visitor comes into our midst, what often
compels them to return is the quality of the preaching and
the welcome of the people. Too often in the small church,
however, we expect visitors to respond to our friendliness
regardless of the quality of the worship and preaching. If this
is true for your church, I'll ask you to think of this: there
are many "friendly" churches out there; unfortunately, there
are fewer churches that provide inspiring, biblical preaching.
Our commitment should be to offer both.

Yet, this does not simply mean being dedicated to
preaching and teaching, although these areas of ministry

should never be neglected or underemphasized. As the apostle Paul instructs us all, as he speaks to the elders at Ephesus, the Word of God is given "in public and from house to house" (Acts 28:20). This means that sharing the truth of Scripture is not only the task of preaching but is also a prominent component of all pastoral care. In fact, as some have said, "Shepherding is synonymous with pastoral care. It is the practical, individual, and spiritual care of Christ's people."[87] Whether a pastor is preaching on Sunday morning, teaching a Bible study on Tuesday evening, visiting someone in the hospital on Thursday afternoon, counseling another person in their home on Friday morning, or is a guest in the home of a church member for a BBQ on Saturday, she or he is in position to feed the Lord's sheep by the Word of God.

This takes place by word and by personal example. The apostle Paul commanded the believers at Corinth, "Be imitators of me, as I am of Christ" (1 Cor 11:1). The apostle Peter called upon all church leaders to be "examples to the flock" (1 Pt 5:3). This activity grows believers and equips the church by providing a continuing presence and spiritual nourishment well beyond Sunday mornings. As you can see, feeding the flock should occur not only in the church building but also "out in the field" where the people of God live and work, raise their children, and serve in their community.

---

[87] Prime and Begg, 143.

LEAD

When a pastor is engaged in activities that heed and feed the flock as their pastor, they are then in a position to more confidently and effectively *lead* them. One import- ant key to leadership is serving as an example, an aspect of ministry already seen under feeding the church, but it is just as valid here. If members of the church are going to understand their own "ministry" in terms of "service" then their pastor must be an example of true servanthood. In a similar way, if the pastor is going to train other leaders in the church, then the pastor must demonstrate exactly what that looks like in their own servant-leadership of the church.

This being said, this leadership is directed in fulfill- ing the mission of the church to make disciples through worship, discipleship, fellowship, and evangelism. This is a leading in word and deed as the pastor both models this in their own life and calls other to join them—providing a vision of what God desires of us all. As Glenn Daman has said, "The church's greatest need today, in terms of leadership, is men and women who have a biblical un- derstanding of what God desires the church to become as both a reflection of the person of Christ and a dynamic influence in the world."[88] To this end, the pastor as leader, particularly in a smaller church, will at the very least assist

---

[88] Daman, 126-127.

the congregation in focusing on mission priorities, establishing and empowering a biblical model of ministry for elders and deacons, setting up effective ministry structures (perhaps simplifying those that are already in place) and clarifying the expectations and priorities of the church and the pastor.

NEED

Crucial to everything that has been said about the necessity to heed, feed, and lead the church as shepherds of the flock is the recognition that, above everything else, pastors are also sheep in *need* of care.[89] In Acts 20:28, the apostle Paul tells us, "Pay careful attention to yourselves and to all the flock, in which the Holy Spirit has made you overseers, to care for the church of God, which he obtained with his own blood." What is clear from this passage is that, in order to care for the church, pastors need to devote attention to their own spiritual life and health as well.

In the Bible, a pastor is instructed to "train yourself in godliness" (1 Tim 4:7), "to set an example in speech, in conduct, in love, in faith, in purity" (1 Tim 4:12), to

---

[89] Another way of looking at this is with the image of the body of Christ. See: Paul David Tripp, *Dangerous Calling: Confronting the Unique Challenges of Pastoral Ministry* (Wheaton, IL: Crossway, 2012), 88. Tripp makes this helpful point: "I think of it this way: if Christ is the head of his body, then everything else is just body, including the pastor, and therefore the pastor needs what the body has been designed to deliver."

"pursue righteousness, godliness, faith, love, steadfastness, gentleness" (1 Tim 6:11) to "hold firmly to the trustworthy word as taught" (Titus 1:9), and to be models of "good works" (Titus 2:7), among other things. Paying careful attention, therefore, to living a life of prayer and dependence upon the Lord, keeping a Sabbath for ourselves, protecting time with family and friends, pursuing passions and interests that refresh and revitalize our body and soul, and utilizing all the means of grace God richly and graciously supplies through the church, is a vital task of every shepherd.[90] In fact, all the tasks—to heed, feed, lead, and need—depend upon and complement one another. All should be expected of every shepherd, including part-time pastors.

These are all part of a part-time pastor's calling, the life and work that they should be expected by their churches to fulfill. By focusing on these areas of pastoral ministry, the local church will be built up and equipped for her own mission in this world to "make disciples" who, growing in faith and maturity in Christ, each fulfill their own calling as Christians in this life. By answering this call of God, we may all be faithful and fruitful disciples of Jesus Christ.

---

[90] For an in-depth look at the *need* of a pastor, see: Michael Todd Wilson and Brad Hoffman, *Preventing Ministry Burnout* (Downer's Grove, IL: InterVarsity, 2007).

QUESTIONS FOR REFLECTION

1. *What is the "purpose" of the pastor of your church?*

2. *If you were to make a job description for your pastor, what do you think must absolutely belong on the list of duties and responsibilities?*

3. *How important is sound, biblical preaching to your church?*

4. *For the shepherd model of ministry presented above—heed, feed, lead, need—which of these do you think is most important? Why?*

5. *What kind of care does your pastor need from your congregation?*

Part Three:

A PARTNERSHIP IN
FULL-TIME MINISTRY

Chapter 5
MUTUAL EXPECTATIONS

One of the greatest areas of frustration in the life of a pastor is often the unrealistic expectations that churches place upon them. This is also one of the primary sources of conflict and disappointment, straining their relationship and undermining their ability to work effectively together. This goes both ways.

Pastors, too, can hold their churches to expectations that range from farcical to fanatical. One pastor I know expected his congregation to supply the toilet paper for the parsonage he was living in with his family. Another pastor I know expected every member of his church to follow his vision for the church without hesitation, question or debate. After all, "God told him" what they needed to do, so that was that!

Way too often, the real difficulty lies in the fact that most expectations for the pastor and the church are un-spoken—or simply assumed. This is true even during a search process for a part-time pastor. Churches may give their pastoral candidate the impression that they only want her to preach on Sundays, visit them in the hospital when they get sick, and offer pastoral care for their members when needed. Then, soon after she begins her ministry with them, she discovers that the adult Sunday School is expecting her to lead their class every Sunday, the women's group would like her to offer a devotion at their meeting "when she has time" to spend with them, the consistory is asking her when she plans to start a youth ministry at their church, and the congregation believes that everyone who is either related to someone in the church or someone that they care about is to be treated as a "member" of the church and is expected to receive hospital visits, pastoral counseling, wedding and funeral services, and all the rest. The reality is: A "part-time" call to a small church of 50 members has now become for her a call to a much larger church of over 150 souls, and counting.

Needless to say, this is not what she signed up for! Even more, it is an impossible ministry for her to carry out well—especially while also needing to work another paid position outside the church, 24 hours a week or more, in order to make ends meet. Neither this pastor, nor her church, were satisfied with the end result. Yet, the situation I just described to you is a true story. And many more like it can be told.

THE EXPECTATIONS OF THE CHURCH

So, what should a church expect from their part-time pastor? I suggest, at the very least, all the following:

- **Your pastor will be a person of strong character.** In the Bible, the qualifications for a pastor overwhelming stress a spiritual giftedness for ministry and the quality of his or her character. If your pastor is going to be an example for the congregation, be authentic and believable when they share the Word of God, be someone the congregation can respect and follow in leadership, and be an attractive representative of the church in the community, then personal integrity is an absolute necessity.

- **Your pastor will sense God's calling to bivocational ministry.** This is a specific call—to this unique form of ministry—for your particular church—in loving response to God's will for their life. They are not looking to be anyone else, or serve anywhere else. They will not settle for anything less than what God desires for them, even if it is a bigger church with greater status for more money.

- **Your pastor will believe and preach the Word of God.** It is God who creates, nourishes, grows and leads His church through His divine Word. No church will be healthy and grow, in either spiritual depth or numerical strength, without a devotion and obedience to the Bible.

- **Your pastor will be a person of prayer.** No pastor is able to lead or care for the church on their own. No pastor has the wisdom or strength, or has enough love or patience, equal to the task. It is too great—and too holy—for a mere mortal to handle. Your pastor needs the power and presence of God that only comes through the grace of prayer.

- **Your pastor will love the people of the church.** Everyone in the congregation, and every person in the community, will we be known by your pastor as those who God so loves that Jesus suffered and died on the cross for their sake. This love will flow through and direct their ministry and be clearly evident in their life.

- **Your pastor will provide pastoral care to the church.** This is a ministry of presence as much as it is a sharing of biblical truth, comfort, teaching and correction. Time and attention should be intentionally devoted to this needed ministry.

- **Your pastor will provide leadership to the church.** This will be done mutually and cooperatively with the other designated leaders of the church. The mission of the church will be kept in sharp focus while specific programs and goals appropriate for your church will be initiated.

- **Your pastor will train people for ministry.** This includes the instruction and development of elders and deacons as well as teaching and training the members of the congregation to utilize their gifts for ministry.

- **Your pastor will agree upon the duties and expectations of their ministry with the church**. This will begin with conversations with the search committee, be followed by honest discussions with the consistory, and then forever be communicated to the entire congregation. These responsibilities must be well-defined, designating not only what is expected of the pastor, but also articulating specifically what is not—like not requiring the pastor to attend ecumenical events, to be present at all the church suppers, or to preside over budget committee meetings.

This does not mean, of course, that part-time pastors should never be expected to teach adult Sunday School classes, attend ecumenical events, order the church supplies for worship, make copies of the Sunday bulletin, or complete a variety of other needed tasks for the church. Someone has to do these things. Yet, it all depends upon what has been mutually agreed upon as the specific responsibilities of your pastor.

Additionally, the actual amount of time the pastor is expected to serve within the church must be considered. And valued. If the pastor is expected to start a youth group in the church, for example, then it is likely that something else—like leading a mid-week Bible study or taking communion to the shut-ins—has to be sacrificed, or someone else has to assume ownership for that need. This is only being fair to your part-time pastor. A church should honor the fact that they have *not* called a full-time pastor.

The Expectations of the Part-Time Pastor

Every pastor has expectations for their church. And they are not always biblical or realistic. When I first became a pastor, I was extremely disappointed to find that my church didn't hang on my every word, wasn't always eager to love their neighbor as themselves, didn't believe I walked on water, and wasn't always nice to one another (not even to me!). But the problem wasn't them; the problem was me. They were simply being the people of God—sinners saved by grace—and needing to grow, day by day, into the likeness of Jesus Christ. In other words, my problem was that my church members were just like me. But I expected more from them.

So, what should a part-time pastor expect from their church? Here is what I suggest:

- **The church will pray for their part-time pastor.** As I said earlier, your pastor needs God's help to be an effective servant-leader to the church. Even more, just knowing that people in the church are personally committed to praying for them is often the greatest source of encouragement, support, and blessing you can give them.

- **The church will accept the leadership of their part-pastor.** Some small churches are reluctant to share leadership with their pastor. They may have had a steady stream of short-term ministers in the past; they may have experienced such a long period of time between pastors that other leadership has emerged, leadership that will not step down or let anyone else assume authority; or they may resist the leadership of their new pastor until, at some time in the far-distant future, their pastor somehow proves worthy of their trust. But few pastors will remain long at a church that will not listen to their suggestions, take seriously their ideas, or share their vision for the church.

- **The church will care for their part-time pastor and family.** Like the other members of your church, your pastor and their family need the love and care of your community of faith. They have stresses and problems, issues and challenges, the need to belong and be appreciated—just like every other family in the church. Sometimes even more so, given the high expectations that are often placed upon them.

- **The church will have realistic expectations for their part-time pastor.** No pastor can complete a day's work and rest easy that there is nothing further that needs to be done. There is worship to plan, a sermon to prepare, a meeting to get ready for, a Bible study to work on, people to pray for, hospital visits to be made, phone calls to return, e-mails to read, and supper to make. I'm sure I am forgetting something. This is even more challenging for a bivocational pastor. Knowing truly what is expected, from week to week, season to season, is absolutely necessary.

- **The church will serve as ministers alongside their part-time pastor.** This includes elders and deacons fulfilling their role as outlined in the Scriptures along with other members of the congregation stepping up and using their gifts for the benefit of others.

- **The church will understand their pastor is part-time.** This means they are willing to give and receive ministry in the church from someone other than their pastor. Also, it means they will recognize that there will be times when their pastor is not immediately available to them, so more flexibility and grace will be required from them by their pastor.

- **The church will support the work of ministry with their attendance and giving.** The church is only as useful to God as we are willing to give our time, talents, and treasure to His service. Nothing energizes a pastor more than seeing the enthusiasm of their congregation for worship and contributing to the mission and growth of the church.

- **The church will do their best to pay their part-time pastor.** This means that the church will attempt to compensate their pastor the best they can, not the least they can. Sometimes I get the impression that, during discussions about salary, some church leaders are actually trying to purchase a pastor for the cheapest price possible—like buying a used car. (What's the old saying?—"You get what you pay for!") It is often very obvious and disheartening for the pastor. Instead, the church should prayerfully consider what is the most they can pay their pastor in salary, housing, health coverage and the like, being as flexible and creative as possible, and then tell their pastoral candidates that they are doing just this. That church, which demonstrates its desire to give their very best to their new pastor, will most likely receive the very best from new pastor in return. It is an honorable way to begin in ministry together.

Questions for Reflection

1. *Are the "Expectations of the Church" listed above appropriate and realistic?*

2. *Would you add or subtract anything? What is it and why?*

3. *Are the "Expectations of the Part-Time Pastor" appropriate and realistic?*

4. *Would you add or subtract anything? What is it and why?*

5. *How would you share these with your congregation?*

Chapter 6
THE ESSENTIALS

I don't believe gospel ministry is all that complicated. It is not easy, but it certainly is not complicated. In fact, it is pretty straight-forward. As we've discussed, as Christians we have all been called to salvation in Jesus Christ and have been given the command by our Lord and Savior to "make disciples." We have even been instructed in how we are to go about this: Worship, Fellowship, Discipleship, and Evangelism. God has even provided pastors, elders, deacons and fellow believers to help us to grow and to fulfill our purpose. He has joined us together as His church to live and work with one another for our good and for His glory. Like I said, there is nothing complicated about this.

We can make ministry harder than it should be. God has revealed to us a simple plan, but we—especially church leaders—are inclined to seek new ways, new ideas, new programs, new inventions, new procedures, new "paradigms" (I hate this word) in order to improve upon (I'm being kind) or get around (I'm being less kind) what God has called us to do. The result is almost always a real mess.

We miss the mark we were aiming for. Why? We lose sight of who we are, what we are trying to accomplish and, all too often, who we are called to serve—Christ and His church.

I hope that what I have presented so far has not made a mess of things. Calling a part-time pastor is not that complicated. Yes, it takes a great deal of time, effort, and cooperation; but that is true of all Christian endeavors. Yes, it does require a right understanding of the biblical teachings on the mission of the church, the role of pastor, and the ministry of all believers; but that is just basic theology every Christian should know, anyway. And, of course, it does rely upon prayer and the leading of the Holy Spirit, and paying attention to how the Word of God directs us to proceed; which is common Christian practice after all. This is all I have tried to follow.

In light of this, what follows is what I hope to be an uncomplicated summary of what this entire work has been about. These are the essential areas that need careful attention in order to provide and maintain a healthy relationship between a church and their part-time pastor. There are 7 of them, all beginning with the letter "C" in order to help you remember them. I call them the "7 C's" for calling a part-time pastor. I know some of my colleagues will laugh at me for choosing to use alliteration here (I can hear you, Fred and Steve!), but I have found this system helpful as I worked through this subject, so I present it to you this simple way.

1. CHRIST

Always remember, your church belongs to Jesus. You belong to Jesus. He alone is the Head of the Church. He is the true leader in the church. As you are calling a pastor, know that you already have a leader for the church. Christ is present with you now. And even after you call a part-time pastor, Jesus will still be the *full-time leader* of the church. Having a pastor doesn't change this.

Also remember, Jesus declared, "I will build my church" (Mat 16:18). Although we all should desire a growing church and faithfully work for a growing church—to *make disciples*—ultimately the outcome rests in the will of God. Our task is to be faithful to our calling, whatever size we are right now, trusting that Christ will do the rest according to His good pleasure.

The part-time pastor you seek to call will have a personal relationship with Jesus Christ. Their life and ministry will be led by a great love and devotion for our Savior, a joyful obedience to our Lord, and a passionate commitment to His church. Everything else about your pastor and their ministry with you will proceed from this vital relationship with Christ. Therefore, let me emphasize, all church leaders will do well to inquire at length about the faith and life of every pastoral candidate.

2. CALLING

Your pastor should feel a calling to a part-time ministry. This is not something they are just doing because they can't find a full-time call. They know this is precisely what they are meant to do. They are even willing to work another job in order to be able to serve a smaller church that may not be able to afford to have a pastor with them otherwise.

Even more, they sense a calling to serve with your particular church in ministry. This is the people and place that your pastor believes would truly please God for him or her to serve among, using the gifts and training that God has provided to build up and equip the church for works of ministry. A search committee should hear a pastoral candidate articulate this sense of calling to serving as a bivocational pastor with a church like your church. It needs to be apparent that a particular candidate for your ministry is "all in" and is not just biding time with you, waiting for something else to open up or some other opportunity to come their way.

In the same way, the church must also understand that you are called to a ministry with a part-time pastor at this time in your church's history. The fact that Christ is calling a pastor to serve in your church is proof that God has good intentions for your church. That God has plans for your church. That perhaps the best years of your church may not be in the past, but just ahead, in ways you can't even imagine.

3. Confidence

There are many churches today that are served by part-time pastors. Tens of thousands of them in the United States alone. Even countless more throughout the world. And very many of them are healthy, thriving, and sharing the good news of salvation with their neighbors. These are good, faithful churches. Biblical churches. Churches we can be sure God is working through, and we would be excited to be a part of, no matter what size they are right now.

Church history, our history, is filled with these small, vital and hopeful congregations. God has always done mighty things through them. Some would say that small churches have been the primary way God has been saving people all throughout the years. And, if what we see in small churches today is any indication, I don't believe this is going to change anytime soon. In truth, we can be confident that God can use even the smallest, weakest vessel on earth to do great things in His name. The Bible says He has been doing just that, through us, right from the beginning (1 Cor 1:26-31).

4. Clarity

Focus. Focus. Focus. It must be kept, first of all, on your mission as a church. Nothing should be allowed to distract or side-track you from the purpose for which you were called—to make disciples. This mission should be clear to the congregation, to the pastor being called, and to every other leader in the church, especially to those directly involved in calling your new pastor. After all, if you don't know why the church exists, what are we calling a pastor help you to do? What do you plan to achieve together?

Focus should also be concentrated on formulating *appropriate* and *realistic* expectations for your part-time pastor and the church. The "job description" should not be vague but highly specific, from the number of Sundays a year the pastor should preach and even down to the amount of time each week the pastor is expected to spend on sermon preparation, "office work" or home visitation. This then needs to be communicated widely to the whole congregation in an effort to avoid, as best we possibly can, any misunderstandings and hurt feelings between some members of the church and the pastor.

5. COOPERATION

Every church has a full-time ministry, and then some. This means that your pastor and every member of your church must each do their part. For a church that has a part-time pastor, this is even more urgent and essential. Leaders especially, meaning elders and deacons, have to step up to the plate and assume their biblical roles and responsibilities.

Collaboration will be the key to being a strong church.

You will serve together well to the extent that ministry will be shared according to every person's calling, when everyone in leadership acknowledges the God-given position of everyone else, as an atmosphere of mutual respect and humility governs all leadership meetings, as a culture of honest and open communication is expected between your pastor and other leaders, and when service in the name of the Lord is encouraged for every member of your church. In other words, we as leaders, and as Christians, should conduct ourselves in manner worthy of the gospel of Jesus Christ (Phil 1:27). In this way, "the priesthood of all believers" will be built up in your church.

In addition, even before a new pastor arrives, the other leaders of the church need to decide to what extent they will honor the person they call as the "pastor" of the church. And they will need to decide to what extent they will allow the person they call as their pastor to "lead" with them. Do they want a true *shepherd* of God, or do they merely want someone to perform the duties they assign to them, without input or question? Will the pastor be given a voice in deliberations? A say in decision-making? A place at the table? I would also advise that, when interviewing pastoral candidates, the church discovers that potential pastor's leadership style and their acceptance of the leadership of others. Do they accept the "priesthood of all believers" as a biblical characteristic of Christ's church?

6. COMPETENCE

As a shepherd for your church, you should require your pastor to be dedicated to some form of *heed, feed, lead,* and *need* model for pastoral ministry. This being said, these words that I use to describe pastoral ministry are not the main point; the mind-set and activities that they portray are what is essential. As you interview a pastoral candidate, they should not be expected to recite this group of words. But what they should be expected to do is tell you what is important to them as a pastor in each of these areas.

I urge church leaders to inquire about a potential pastor's intention to know and love your congregation and community and how they plan to go about this. Also, do they rely upon prayer and the Word of God to guide their ministry? Do they cherish the Bible and are they dedicated to preaching the whole counsel of God? Do they offer personal counsel from the Word of God? You get the idea.

What is at stake, of course, is the spiritual care of your congregation and the health of your church. I believe, any person worthy of the title "pastor" will not only welcome such a conversation, but will be greatly attracted to a church who engages them in a deep discussion about these important matters.

7. COMPENSATION

The main idea here is to be honest, fair, and creative. This pertains to the church and to the pastor. Don't make it a negotiation between two competing parties; instead make it an exploration of the best way to enter into a *partnership in the gospel* together for the benefit of the church. What does this look like? Basically, you all sit down together to come up what is mutually beneficial. Remember, the part-time pastor has already agreed not to be fully compensated by the church, has already committed to working another job to serve your church, and has already relinquished many benefits of serving in a fully-funded ministry (like more time for sermon preparation, more days for visitation, more opportunities to attend conferences and church events, more flexibility in scheduling, and the like). In other words, this pastor has already demonstrated their dedication to serving as a partner in the gospel with you.

You can show your dedication to serving in partnership in the gospel with them by representing the financial position of the church with integrity. One pastor I know was informed by the treasurer of his church that they only had enough money to pay him for next three years, maybe less. He was told this *after* he began his ministry with them.

Another way to show your dedication is to offer what is right, financially speaking, for the amount of ministry you expect of them. If you really expect your pastor to serve in

Warren Seibert

a "full-time" role in terms of hours per week, but you are only offering them compensation equal to "half-time" in terms of hours per week, you being dishonest and unfair. And to call it what it really is: You are sinning against your pastor and against God. Some churches do not intend to do this, but when they realize weeks or months later that this is precisely how this call is turning out, they often ignore it and do nothing about it. This, as you can imagine, is a recipe for disaster.

Here is where creativity must come in. Perhaps you plan on calling a part-time pastor for "1/2" time. Yet your church cannot afford what is required for this. There are other benefits you can offer, rather than money. There may be a parsonage that can be used by the pastor. If the pastor will reside in the parsonage with full utilities paid by the church, but is only going to be "1/2" time, you are already providing a substantial benefit to the pastor. Therefore, the pastor may agree to the salary portion of the compensation being less than usual for "1/2" time. Think also about a pastor who makes a good living at their other job. Maybe being offered more money will not appeal to them as much as being offered more weeks off for vacation or continuing education.

This may pertain to a retired pastor as well. With their pension, their own home, and a fire still in their belly to serve Christ and His church, a retired pastor who desires to serve "part-time" may an incredible find for your church. They have the time, the drive, they don't require a fully-funded setting, and they have many years of experience to offer your church. A retired pastor might be an answer to some church's prayer.

The same is true for a pastor who is already serving part-time in another church in your area and who is willing to receive an additional part-time call. Some small churches will not even consider this option. I don't really understand this. Here, again, is an experienced pastor willing to serve with small churches. Even more, this pastor offers more immediate availability of their time and presence than most other part-time pastors who are working a "secular" job. In fact, the only time this pastor will be unavailable to your church members is when they are leading worship on Sunday morning at their other church. You can't say that about me, for example. I work as an RN. And when I am working as an RN, I am definitely not available to the people of my church until my shift is over. All this is to say, there is more than money you can offer a potential part-time pastor for your church. In conversation with your candidates, you may discover an option that works well for all of you as you seek to begin your partnership in the gospel.

Truly, church leaders who pay attention to these essential areas of part-time ministry will serve their church well. They will honor their own calling to serve Christ and His church to the very best of their ability and affection. And they will look forward in faith to enjoying a healthy and fruitful ministry with their new pastor and, most of all, in hopeful expectation of God's blessing upon their church for years to come.

Questions for Reflection

1. *How might you apply these 7 "C's" to your pastoral search process?*

2. *Are there specific questions church leaders could ask potential pastors from each of these essentials categories? What would they be?*

3. *Are there specific questions part-time pastors should ask potential churches from each of these essential categories? What would they be?*

4. *In what ways should supervisors apply these 7 "C's" in their ministry to churches?*

5. *What is the ultimate goal for putting in all this time and attention?*

BIBLIOGRAPHY

Allen, Larry. "Pastoral Leadership and the Bivocational Pastor," *Church Administration* 31, no. 4 (January 1989): 15-16.

Barcley, William B. *1 & 2 Timothy*. Darlington, England: Evangelical Press. 2005.

Bargiol, J. W. "The Bivocational Pastor," *Church Administration* 29, no. 6 (March 1987): 12-15.

Benton, John. *Straightening Out the Self-Centered Church: The Message of Titus*. Durham, England: Evangelical Press, 1997.

Berkoff, Louis. *Systematic Theology*. Carlisle, PA: Banner of Truth Trust, 1958.

Bickers, Dennis W. *The Bivocational Pastor: Two Jobs, One Ministry*. Kansas City, MO: Beacon Hill Press, 2004.

---- *The Healthy Small Church: Diagnosis and Treatment for the Big Issues.* Kansas City, MO: Beacon Hill Press, 2005.

---- *The Work of a Bivocational Minister.* Valley Forge, PA: Judson Press, 2007.

Bierly, Steven R. *How to Thrive as a Small Church Pastor: A Guide to Spiritual and Emotional Well-Being.* Grand Rapids, MI: Zondervan, 1998.

Bridges, Jerry. *The Pursuit of Holiness.* Colorado Springs, CO: NavPress, 1996.

Brouwer, Arie R. *Reformed Church Roots.* Grand Rapids, MI: Eerdmans, 1977.

Brown, Willard Dayton. *History of the Reformed Church in America.* New York: Board of Publication and Bible School Work, 1928.

Brug, John F. "Doctrinal Brief: Part-Time Pastors," *Wisconsin Lutheran Quarterly* 105, no. 3 (Summer 2008): 222-228.

Callahan, Kennon L. *Small, Strong Congregations: Creating Strengths and Health for Your Congregation.* San Francisco, CA: Jossey-Bass, 2000.

Calvin, John. *Institutes of the Christian Religion.* Translated by Henry Beveridge. Peabody, MA: Hendrickson, 2008.

Christian Reformed Church. *More Than a Search Committee.* Grand Rapids, MI: Christian Reformed Church, 2012.

Clowney, Edmund P. *Called to Ministry.* Phillisburg, NJ: P&R, 1964.

--- *The Church.* Downers Grove, IL: InterVarsity, 1995.

Coughlin, Michael E. "Full-time Pastor, Part-time Pay," *Leadership* 12, no. 2 (Spring 1991): 111-113.

Daman, Glenn C. *Leading the Small Church: How to Develop a Transformational Ministry.* Grand Rapids, MI: Kregel, 2006.

De Jong, Gerald F. *The Dutch Reformed Church in the American Colonies.* Grand Rapids, MI: Eerdmans, 1978.

De Moor, Robert. *Reformed: What It Means, Why It Matters.* Grand Rapids, MI: Faith Alive, 2009.

DeYoung, Kevin. *The Hole in Our Holiness: Filling the Gap Between Gospel Passion and The Pursuit of Godliness.* Wheaton, IL: Crossway, 2012.

DeYoung, Kevin and Greg Gilbert. *What Is the Mission of the Church: Making Sense Of Social Justice, Shalom, and the Great Commission*. Wheaton, IL: Crossway, 2011.

Dever, Mark. *The Church: The Gospel Made Visible*. Nashville, TN: B & H Academic, 2012.

--- *What Is a Healthy Church?" Making Sense of Shalom, Social Justice, and the Great Commission*. Wheaton, IL: Crossway, 2007

Dingman, Robert W. *In Search of a Leader: The Complete Search Committee Guidebook*. Ventura, CA: Regal Books, 1989.

Doriani, Daniel M. *Matthew, Vol. 2: Chapters 14-28*. Phillipsburg, NJ: P & R Publishing, 2008.

Dorr, Luther M. *The Bivocational Pastor*. Nashville, TN: Broadman, 1988.

Dorsett, Terry W. *Developing Leadership Teams in the Bivocational Church*. Bloomington, IL: CrossBooks, 2010.

Elder, Gregory P. "The Challenge of Part-time Ministry," *Christian Ministry* 18, no. 2 (March 1987): 28-29.

Fasol, Al. "Bivocational Ministers Need These Qualities," *Church Administration* 29, no. 6 (March 1987): 9-11.

Ferguson, Sinclair B. *The Christian Life: A Doctrinal Introduction.* Carlisle, PA: Banner of Truth, 1989.

Gaede, Beth Ann, ed. *Size Transitions in Congregations.* Baltimore, MD: Alban Institute, 2001.

Gilbert, David L. *The Candidate Evaluation Process: An Investigation of Pastoral Candidate.* Lancaster Bible College: Directed Research Project, 2000.

Gilder, Ray. *Uniquely Bivocational: Understanding the Life of a Pastor Who Has a Second Job.* Forest, VA: Salt & Light Publishing, 2013.

Grenz, Stanley J. *Theology for the Community of God.* Nashville, TN: Broadman & Holman, 1994.

Guinness, Os. *The Call: Finding and Fulfilling the Central Purpose of Your Life.* Nashville, TN: Thomas Nelson, 2003.

Guthrie, Donald. *The Pastoral Epistles.* Downers Grove, IL: InterVarsity, 1990

Hageman, Howard G. *Lily Among the Thorns.* New York: Half Moon Press, 1953.

Hager, Donald A. *Matthew 1-13: Word Biblical Commentary.* Nashville, TN: Thomas Nelson, 1993.

Hartford Seminary. "2010 Faith Communities Today Survey," in MacDonald, G. Jeffery. "Churches Turn to Part-time Clergy," *Christian Century.* (September 13, 2013).

Harvey, Dave. *Am I Called? The Summons to Pastoral Ministry.* Wheaton, IL: Crossway, 2012.

Head, K. Maynard. "The Call to Bivocational Ministry," *Church Administration* 29, no. 6 (March 1987): 7-8.

Horton, Michael. *The Christian Faith: A Systematic Theology for Pilgrims On the Way.* Grand Rapids, MI: Zondervan, 2011.

Laniak, Timothy S. *Shepherds After My Own Heart: Pastoral Traditions and Leadership in the Bible.* Downers Grove, IL: InterVarsity, 2006.

---*While Shepherds Watch Their Flock: Rediscovering Biblical Leadership.* Matthews, NC: Shepherd Leader Publications, 2007.

LaRochelle, Robert. *Part-Time Pastor, Full-Time Ministry.* Cleveland, OH: Pilgrim Press, 2010.

Liefeld, Walter L. *1 & 2 Timothy and Titus.* Grand Rapids, MI: Zondervan, 1999.

Lummis, Adair T. *What Do Lay People Want in a Pastor? Answers from Lay Search Committee Chairs and Regional Judicatory Leaders.* Durham, NC: Duke Divinity School, 2003.

Luther, Martin. *The Babylonian Captivity of the Church.* N.P.: FigBooks, 2012. Kindle.

Macchia, Stephen A. *Becoming a Healthy Church: 10 Traits of a Vital Ministry.* Grand Rapids, MI: Baker, 1999.

MacNair, Donald. *The Practices of a Healthy Church.* Phillipsburg, NJ: P & R Publications, 1999.

Marshal, Colin and Tony Payne. *The Trellis and the Vine.* Kingsford, Australia: Matthias Media, 2009.

Migliore, Daniel L. *Faith Seeking Understanding: An Introduction to Christian Theology.* Grand Rapids, MI: Eerdmans, 1991.

Minear, Paul. *Images of the Church in the New Testament.* Philadelphia, PA: Westminster, 1960.

Motyer, J. A. *The Message of Philippians.* Downers Grove, IL: InterVarsity, 1984.

Mounce, William E. *Pastoral Epistles.* Nashville, TN: Thomas Nelson, 2000.

Norcross, Stephen. "The Bivocational Option." In *Inside the Small Church,* edited by Anthony Pappas, 56-68. Baltimore, MD: Alban Institute, 2002.

O'Brien, Brandon J. *The Strategically Small Church.* Minneapolis, MN: Bethany House, 2010.

O'Brien, Peter T. *The Letter to the Ephesians.* Grand Rapids, MI: Eerdmans, 1999.

Osterhouse, Jim. *Faith Unfolded: A Fresh Look at the Reformed Faith.* Grand Rapids, MI: Faith Alive, 2000.

Oswald, Roy, "How to Minister Effectively in Family, Pastoral, Program and Corporate Sized Churches." In *Size Transitions in Congregations,* edited by Beth Ann Gaede, 31-46. Baltimore, MD: Alban Institute, 2001.

Packer, J. I. *Rediscovering Holiness: Know the Fullness of Life with God.* Ventura, CA: Regal, 2009.

Pappas, Anthony G. *Entering the World of the Small Church: A Guide for Leaders.* Baltimore, MD: Alban Institute, 1988.

--- *Inside the Small Church.* Baltimore: Alban Institute, 2002.

Prime, Derek J., and Alistair Begg. *On Being a Pastor: Understanding Our Calling and Work.* Chicago, IL: Moody, 2004.

Ray, David R. *The Indispensable Guide for Smaller Churches.* Cleveland, OH: Pilgrim Press, 2003.

Reeder, Harry III. *From Embers to a Flame.* Phillipsburg, NJ: P & R Publishing, 2004.

Reformed Church in America. *The Acts and Proceedings of the 198th Regular Session of the General Synod,* 2004.

---- *Book of Church Order,* 2014.

---- *Pastoral Search Handbook,* 2004.

Richards, Lawrence O. *Encyclopedia of Bible Words*. Grand Rapids, MI: Zondervan, 1991.

Ryken, Philip Graham. *1 Timothy: Reformed Expository Commentary*. Phillipsburg, NJ: P & R Publishing, 2007.

Ryle, John Charles. *Holiness*. Webster, NY: Evangelical Press, 1979.

Schaller, Lyle E. *The Small Membership Church: Scenarios for Tomorrow*. Nashville, TN: Abingdon, 1994.

Smallman, Stephen. *What Is Discipleship?* Phillipsburg, NJ: P & R Publishing, 2011.

Smietetara, Bob. "More Preachers Need a Day Job, Too." *USA Today,* February 29, 2010. Accessed April 27, 2013. http://www.usatoday.com/news/religion/2010-06-21-preachers20_ST_N.htm.

Spradling, Robert K. and Warren W. Wiersbe. *The Lost Shepherd: Finding and Keeping The Right Shepherd*. Grand Rapids, MI: Discovery House, 2008.

Stott, John. *The Living Church: Convictions of a Lifelong Pastor*. Downers Grove, IL: InterVarsity, 2007.

--- *Basic Christianity*. Grand Rapids, MI: Eerdmans, 1998.

---*The Message of Ephesians.* Downer's Grove, IL: InterVarsity, 1979.

---*The Message of 1 Timothy and Titus.* Downer's Grove, IL: InterVarsity, 1996.

The Holy Bible: English Standard Version. Wheaton, IL: Crossway, 2001.

Tripp, Paul David. *Dangerous Calling: Confronting the Unique Challenges of Pastoral Ministry.* Wheaton, IL: Crossway, 2012.

Voskuil, Betty. *The Ministry of the Deacon.* New York: Reformed Church Press, 2003.

Warren, Rick. *The Purpose Driven Church: Growth Without Compromising Your Message and Mission.* Grand Rapids, MI: Zondervan, 1995.

Webster's II New College Dictionary. Boston, MA: Houghton Mifflin, 2001.

White, Robert. *The Ministry of the Elder.* New York: Reformed Church Press, 1996.

Wilkins, Michael J. *Matthew: The NIV Application Commentary.* Grand Rapids, MI: Zondervan, 2004.

Wilson, Michael Todd and Brad Hoffmann. *Preventing Ministry Failure*. Downer's Grove, IL: InterVarsity, 2007.

Witmer, Timothy Z. *The Shepherd Leader: Achieving Effective Shepherding in Your Church*. Phillipsburg, NJ: P & R Publishing, 2010.

Printed in the United States
By Bookmasters